IN THE LAP

OF THE GODS

AND THE HANDS

OF THE

BEATLES

Alan Parker
David F Bowles
Keith Bateson

PUBLISHED BY ARCHWAY PUBLISHING COMPANY
IN CONJUNCTION WITH
G.C.P. PUBLICATIONS
BCM BOX 3595, LONDON WC1 3XX

FIRST PUBLISHED 1990

© BATESON BOWLES LTD.

BRITISH LIBRARY IN CATALOGUING IN PUBLICATION DATA
Parker, Alan, 1965-
In the Lap of the Gods and the Hands of the Beatles.
1. Pop music. Beatles.
1. Title II. Bateson, Keith, 1940- III. Bowles, David, 1952-
781.630922

I.S.B.N. 1 853880 03 5

TYPESET AND PRINTED BY
NEWMAN THOMSON LTD, BRIGHTON, SUSSEX

DEDICATED TO
DOCTOR WINSTON O'BOOGIE
APOLLO C. VERMOUTH
HARRI O'GEORGERSON
AND
OGNIR RRATS

CONTENTS

When I was a young child I was always collecting things - my room had everything from comics with every issue all neat and tidy in a pile, to toy cars all 'parked up' in neat little rows. Nothing for me was ever out of place. I knew always where everything was (I don't think that has ever changed) and I was organised - or was I.?

I remember the first record I ever bought - "Blockbuster" by The Sweet. Later that same year I attended my first Rock Concert at the ripe old age of TEN ! - with my Dad, Uncle and brother (only eight) to chaperone me; Slade were playing live at Blackburn's King George's Hall.

As a child "Starsky and Hutch" were the heroes of the day, every fan (it seemed like everybody I knew) had a black and white roll-neck pullover - FANDOM had arrived!

Actually I now realise that 'Fandom' has been with me all my life in one form or another, but it was only when music came into my life that I understood what true Fandom really meant. Every teenager listens to Music. It can't be avoided - Rock, Punk, Soul, Rap, Disco, you can go on forever as there is always something for everybody. But ask yourself this:

Has an Album ever affected you so much that it changed your life ?

If you can't answer 'Yes' to that question then some of what will follow may come as a shock - or at least be a little hard to swallow.

I was eighteen years of age, working in a menswear shop, engaged, happy, and making plans for the future - what more could a young guy want, right ? WRONG !

Amongst my things there was an Album called "Sgt. Pepper's Lonely Hearts Club Band" and a book about the life of John Lennon (a gift from my fiancee). Oh, they'd been there a while, lurking in the back of my cupboards; that is until one fateful day when we decided to go on a trip to Liverpool, fifty miles away.

During that visit, I might as well have gone through a time warp for I was hit by 'something' which was to affect the rest of my forseeable life, something that had affected millions like me TWENTY YEARS earlier - BEATLEMANIA !

And when it hit, boy, did it hit !

Within six months my life changed completely - engagement off, job change, weekly trips to Liverpool. Life was upside down again, but this time for me turned out to be the right reasons.

Oh, I'm not saying that I didn't make any mistakes (don't we all) and I do owe one or two apologies. So to those people here they are in print - "Sorry from the bottom of my heart - it may not count for much now, but it means more than it ever could have then!"

As time moved on, records and books turned to compact discs and videos and it wasn't long before I became the owner of what is reputed to be the largest collection of Beatles Memorabilia and rare music/interviews in Europe. One day (when I can afford it) perhaps the collection will be up in bright lights for all to see and enjoy.

But it has been through FABS that perhaps my greatest thrills have been achieved.

Meeting Paul McCartney was like meeting the man from next door - friendly, happy, good to get on with, and for a fan to receive a birthday present from George Harrison was out of this world !

Gradually both my knowledge and associations expanded throughout a period in which many other unbelievable things have happened - including the day a lady rang me up from an estate agency in London. Apparently they were selling the flat which Ringo had passed on to John and rang EMI for some information about the place.

EMI's reply ? "I'm sorry we can't help you. But ring Alan Parker, if anybody knows anything he will!"

It was then that I knew this book should be written, not only for us but for all those fans and readers worldwide who are helping to keep the 'legend' of The Beatles alive. But it took Keith Bateson (who held Ring's glass in the old days - in joke!) and then David Bowles to help us put the information and all our ideas into

words, and the words into "The Lap of the Gods and the Hands of The Beatles".
(When you pick a title keep it short and sweet - Keith Bateson '89.)

The Beatles totally changed my life and in some small way we hope that this
book (and complementing Radio Series of the same name) will build some bridges,
answer some of your questions, and perhaps even uncover some more Beatlemaniacs

For most people few dreams come true. I'm lucky - mine have!

All the Best.

Alan G. Parker
President - FABS

DAVID F. BOWLES

"What I want is to be creative ... to have a purpose in Life ... to leave something worthwhile behind me when I move on ..."

Those words ring true not only with myself, but probably also with many of you readers.

In our seemingly endless search for our 'inner selves' some of us tend to go through life and life's experiences with a 'come what may' approach, which hopefully leads eventually to a realisation of purpose and (if we are lucky) a meaningful answer to that eternal question - WHY ARE WE HERE ?

The Beatles were lucky, and I feel privileged to have been a part of their era, to have grown up through a fascinating period where progress has seen incredible achievements - from Television to Man landing on the Moon.

No lesser were the changes in music.

Following on from the 40's and the Rock 'n Roll era of Elvis and the 50's, the Pop Music of the 60's and 70's revolutionised music and dance styles, bringing with it a 'new beginning.' At the forefront of this revolution were a Pop Group we now know as a legend in their time - The Beatles had arrived!

In this book (and the complementing Radio Series also available) I hope that we (that is Alan Parker, Keith Bateson and myself) bring to you, the reader, something very special - a collection of memories as well as facts; of personalities as well as media profiles; of understanding and meaning rather than just cold stark headlines.

We all recognise the importance of the role of Music around the World, and hope that both yourselves and the media (like us) will continue to fondly remember the Sixties and Seventies - the era of The Beatles, and of their phenomenal contribution to the World of Music.

DAVID.F.BOWLES.

KEITH BATESON

"I'm not doing the "Omar Khyam Show" in front of an invited audience for the BBC Light Programme unless I have the Effects Boy I want !" Thus spoke Spike Milligan in 1963 in the higher echelon offices of BBC Broadcasting House, Portland Place, London West One.

"But Mr. Milligan ..." pleaded the BBC Executive.

"I'm not having my boys on radio unless I can have the Sound Mixer I want !" Thus spoke Brian Epstein.

"But Mr. Epstein ..." pleaded the Executive.

That Effects Boy and Sound Mixer was me !

As a matter of fact I finished up doing both programmes. But this did not make me particularly popular with the BBC as their criteria for employees included "don't make waves!" and "don't be too good at your job or you'll become an embarrassment !"

I did both ! Consequently they parted company with me in 1970.

But my time with The Beatles was (and is) a treasured one, and it was an amazing coincidence when years later (1989 to be exact) I met Alan G. Parker - the 'Blond Bombshell' as he is affectionately known in the 'business' (not showbusiness - the 2nd hand car business - Sorry Alan !)

I had a commission to write an article for a British magazine on the FABS Club (the official Beatles Fan Club based in UK) and the germ of this idea hatched in downtown Blackburn, Lancashire (home of '4000 Holes from Blackburn' fame - and Alan himself.)

Together with my partner David Bowles (of whom Paul McCartney once said "Who?"), we decided with Alan (President of FABS, if you don't already know!) to launch the Radio Series "In the Lap of the Gods and the Hands of The Beatles" - snappy title that, eh!) and with typical logic, together with our quest for rare original info, this book followed.

My connection with Messrs J,P,G, and R started in 1962 with "Pop Go The Beatles" - their primary intro to the world of BBC Radio.

The original Sound Mixer was an old Etonian called Charles Clark-Maxwell who quite frankly had language problems with those little 'Mersey Chappies.' So I was called in to translate and balance everything. This association then led to the Bank Holiday Specials "From Us to You" which I mixed, and later produced, following up later with "Ticket To Ride" which finally saw the end of all 'live music' radio shows on The Beatles.

I guess I was the only BBC Mixer ever to have a Beatles Easter Special go out on the same day he got married. But Easter Monday 1964 will always be a 'red letter day' - not because it was my first Wedding Day but because 20 million listeners were still scratching their heads as to why throughout the programme Ringo Starr kept interjecting with "Congratulations Keith !"

In 1988/1989 "The Beeb's Lost Beatles Tapes" inspired us to think about doing a 'definitive history.' It is ironic, isn't it, that a Corporation can lose the tapes I made, make a programme about how careless they were, and then give THEMSELVES an award for it - AMAZING ! But then again, so were The Beatles !

KEITH BATESON.

JOHN LENNON

("... I was the Walrus, but now I'm John ...")

John Winston Lennon first glimpsed this world on October 9th 1940, the same day that Hitler was bombing Liverpool. As with many others, his family life was not the happiest - although he was closer to his mother Julia.

His father, Freddie Lennon, (whom John was only to see when he was five years old and then again only when he was famous) was away at sea most of the time and died on April 1st 1976 at the age of 63. His mother Julia was killed when a supposedly 'drunken' driver knocked her down with his car. John, shattered by this, immortalised her in the song "Julia". (See "The White Album.")

Consequently John was mainly brought up by his Aunt Mimi and Uncle George (Stanley).

It's fair to say that such a traumatic childhood would have had an effect on anybody - and John was no different. In later life the young Lennon was (in the eyes of Aunt Mimi, Jim McCartney and Louise Harrison) a bad influence and something of a rebel. But one thing was always certain - from a very early age John was destined to be a Something (i.e. very famous) or a Nothing (i.e. a down and out).

Being strongly linked to the fascination of music, it was Lennon's Quarrymen who eventually became The Beatles. His fate was no doubt signed and sealed as a result of Aunt Mimi's most famous one-liner ...

" A guitar's alright John, but you'll never earn you're living by it!"

- the most classic piece of understatement since Dick Rowe's "Guitar Bands like The Shadows are on their way out !" (See Ch. 1)

Through John came Paul, through Paul came George, and with the later addition of Ringo (following Pete Best's short-lived Beatles career) the 'Fab Four' had arrived; and with them came the Road to Glory!

In the following Chapters events in the progress of The Beatles as a group are depicted year by year (a different year every chapter) as are their musical and private lives.

Over the next twenty years,John was to be a major influence not only on other members of the group but on millions of people worldwide. Along with the other members of the group, his musical ability, talent, foresight and caring for others helped to make The Beatles (and their phenomenal contribution to the world of music) legends in their own lifetimes.

But despite his musical drive and enthusiasm over the decades of the 60's and 70's, John Lennon was also the first Beatle to lose faith in the Fab Four. Indeed, at the time of the movie "How I Won the War" (see Chapter Five) he had already begun to look for a way out; and thus he entered the solo phase of his career.

With his second wife, Yoko Ono, his first solo albums were projects which were classed as 'Avant Garde Art' rather than musical. But they all became collectors items - "Two Virgins" (29th November 1968); "Life With the Lyons" (9th May 1969); the "Wedding Album" (7th November 1969).

So it was, on December 11th 1970, that John's first 'true' solo album appeared - "John Lennon/Plastic Ono Band".

This started the 'solo' ball rolling; thus heralding the beginning of numerous important events in John's life - events that were to cover the next decade - the last decade of John's life.

On March 3rd 1971 the ban placed on all Beatles records by South African Radio was lifted. However, music by John Lennon was still banned.

Later that year (on May 11th 1972) John claimed on live television in the USA that the FBI were tapping his phone.

April Fool's Day 1973 - John issued the album "Mind Games". On it was "Nutopian International Anthem " - a track of total silence.

December 27th 1974 - John (plus May Pang and Julian, his son) spent the day at Disneyworld in the USA, a rare family moment.

John, in fact, had two children born to two different wives. The first, Julian, was born to Cynthia (John's first wife) on April 8th 1963 and was later immortalised in

Hey Jude". At the time of writing the 26 year old (who can look and sound remarkably like his father) is a musical star in his own right with three successful albums behind him.

Sean Taro Ono Lennon (his second son) was born to wife Yoko Ono on October 9th 1975. Being the apple of his father's eye he too was immortalised in more than one song. At the time of writing he too has aspired to the musical and entertainment profession and at the tender age of 14 has already appeared on record and in the movie "Moonwalker" (Michael Jackson).

Cynthia Lennon had always said that John was "... forced to be a part-time father with Julian ..." and after Sean's birth John vowed that he was not going to make the same mistake again. So, in April 1976, John announced his decision to quit the music scene.

It wasn't until August 4th 1980, some five years since his last recording session, that John and Yoko entered The Hit Factory in New York to begin work on another album.

In September (the next month) John announced his 'comeback' to the World's press in a lengthy interview with Playboy magazine (see issue dated September 9th 1980). But without a recording contract John and Yoko couldn't issue any more records. So, on September 22nd 1980 they signed with Geffan Records and November 17th 1980 saw the issue of their album "Double Fantasy".

Andy Peebles (BBC Radio One D.J.) arrived in New York on December 5th to tape a long series of interviews with John and Yoko (all of which took place on December 6th); and listening to these interviews it was easy to see that John was happy to be back and (like the 'old' John) was already making plans and looking forward to the future - but for John the future never came.

On December 8th (1980) John taped an interview for the American Radio Network RKO (now available as the album "The Last Word"). He then travelled back to The Hit Factory where he and Yoko were working on "Walking on Thin Ice". At 11.07 p.m. John and Yoko arrived back at the Dakota Building (their home in New York). As John moved towards the entrance of the building Mark David Chapman walked up and pumped five bullets into him at close range. John cried out "I'm shot !" but by the time the police arrived he was losing a lot of blood. Rather than wait for an ambulance he was rushed to hospital in a police car. During the race to the hospital a detective held John's head on his lap and had asked him "Do you know who you are ?"

"Yes," came the reply, "... I'm John Lennon."

They were to be John Lennon's last known words. He was pronounced dead on arrival.

The following day was one of world grief. Whether you were a fan or not you couldn't have failed to be moved by the news. Just as with millions of American's 20 years earlier when they lost President John F. Kennedy, everybody (even today) seems to remember what they were doing that day.

As for the remaining Beatles and their families - they were thunderstruck !

Paul telephoned Yoko, George issued a press statement on behalf of the group, and Ringo (with wife Barbara) flew to New York to comfort Yoko.

On December 14th 1980 (at 2 p.m. EST/7 p.m. GMT) Yoko asked the world to observe ten minutes silence for John - and it is in this tenth anniversary year of John's death that we (the authors) take this opportunity to also offer our own personal condolences (along with those of millions of others) to Yoko and her family as a tribute to John's memory.

As for justice (if there can be any), on August 25th 1981 Mark David Chapman, who had just stood and awaited arrest, was sentenced to twenty years to life by a US Court and was incarcerated at Attica State Prison. During the research period of this book and in the light of the book "The Murder of John Lennon" (Sidgwick & Jackson) Attica State Prison was contacted by the authors to gain some explanation from Chapman (ten years on) for his action. Although the Prison Governor and staff were helpful in advising, Chapman did not respond to our request for an explanation of his action for all those people and Beatles' fans worldwide who were (and still are) unable to comprehend the senselessness of it all.

In the years that have followed, many attacks have been made on John's name and character - indeed none more scathing than that production written by Dr. Albert Goldman and condemned worldwide by The Beatles, their fans and the general public, apparently after also having written a similarly scathing book on Elvis Presley - also after his death !

(NB: Authors' note: Apparently a dead person cannot be slandered or libelled and thus there cannot be any form of legal redress by the dead person or his/her estate or surviving families.)

Whether there be any truth in Dr.Goldman's statements,we(the authors) are not in a position to comment; but,as we feel strongly enough to support any cause that would prevent all/any repetitions of such an intrusion on the memory of persons such as John Lennon-a man who gave so much to the world.

In support of our comments above,the words of supergroup U2's recent hit"God Part II" have been reprinted inside the back of this book with kind permission of U2,their management and Warner Chappell Music(their publishers).Perhaps the words contained therein will sum up some of the feelings and emotions felt worldwide and will go someway towards redressing the balance.

In closing,we also thank Yoko,who is affectionately now known as 'Keeper of the Keys',for her continuing efforts to look after the fans and keep John's memory alive.Since John's death several albums containing hitherto unreleased songs(both,'live' and studio recordings) have been issued along with home videos.It is,however,her two latest projects that have bought the fans the most pleasure-"The Lost Lennon Tapes" and "Imagine-The Movie".

"The Lost Lennon Tapes" is a long running radio series syndicated by Westward One(U.S.A.) and which contains all manner of unissued items-rumoured to follow with a commemorative box set in 1990.

"Imagine-The Movie"(Warners) was the crowning glory of Yoko's more recent tributes to her late husband.It consists of 99 minutes of film,a large percentage seen for the first time ever.

In memory let us never forget his love for music and the world.

GOD PART II

Words by Bono

Music by U2

Don't believe the devil I don't believe his book
but the truth is not the same without the lies he made up
I don't believe in excess 'success is to give'
Don't believe in riches but you should see where I live
I ... I believe in love

Don't believe in forced entry. I don't believe in rape,
but every time she passes by wild thoughts escape.
I don't believe in death row, skidrow or the gangs.
don't believe in the Uzi it just went off in my hand.
I ... I believe in love.

Don't believe in Cocaine I've got a speedboat in my head
I could cut and crack you open ... did you hear what I said.
Don't believe them when they tell me there ain't no cure.
The rich stay healthy, the sick stay poor.

I don't believe in Goldman, his type like a curse.
Instant Karma's gonna get him if I don't get him first.
I don't believe that Rock 'n Roll can really change the world
As it spins in revolution, spirals and turns.

PAUL McCARTNEY

("... Wing Commander ...")

James Paul McCartney was born on June 18th 1942, the eldest son of Jim and Mary McCartney (a second child Michael would arrive in 1944).

By the time he reached school age Paul had already discovered the excitement of music - in particular Rock 'n Roll! However, getting into the music was one thing; dressing accordingly was a different problem entirely.

Paul's father (Jim) was a conservative man who believed a child should be smart at school - being smart meant loose trousers etc. But Paul wasn't going to be defeated, he took them to a local Jewish tailor who, over a period of weeks, gradually took them in until they were narrow enough for Paul's liking.

When Paul later received a guitar as a birthday present (just after the death of his mother Mary McCartney on October 31st 1956 - Rest in Peace) he took it as a way of getting over his mother's passing and went headlong into learning and playing.

But just 'playing' wasn't enough - for young Paul had to know all the words to the songs as well!

In fact it was one of those songs - "Twenty Flight Rock" (with words and music off to a tee) that so much impressed John Lennon (two years his senior) when they first met at a church fete on June 15th 1957. Although impressed, however, it was not like John to give in to anyone at an initial meeting and it was over a week later (when Paul ran into Pete Shotten - another member of John's Quarrymen) that Paul was asked to join the group - and the rest, as they say, is history!

With The Beatles growing in popularity, all members of the group got on well together both personally and musically, and it wasn't long before Paul developed a strong songwriting partnership with John (hence the numerous 'Lennon/McCartney' hits). Their new wave of music along with the continued explosion of Beatlemania across the world over the next decade saw to it that The Beatles became legends in their lifetimes - a unique chapter of Musical History.

Besides developing musically, Paul as a person was also maturing and the next twenty years saw him become not only a part of The Beatles musical sensation, but also eventually develop his own bands and solo career as well as becoming a strong 'family man'.

Paul and his wife Linda currently have four children - Heather (brought to the marriage from Linda's previous divorce, and later adopted by Paul); Mary (born August 29th 1969); Stella (born September 13th 1971) and James (born September 12th 1977).

To be fair Paul's first solo album "The Family Way" which came on December 18th 1966 was an orchestral movie sound-track, and it was not until April 17th 1970 that Paul issued "McCartney" - his first true solo album. Here are some other facts that follow:

On April 14th 1970 Paul obtained full rights to the children's story book star "Rupert Bear".

On August 3rd 1971 Paul and Linda announced the formation of a new band - Wings.

"Give Ireland Back to the Irish" - a new single by Wings was issued on February 25th 1972. But the record was soon to be banned because of the spate of IRA bombings around at that time.

The first proper Wings UK tour opened on May 11th 1973 at the Bristol Hippodrome.

On November 6th 1974 Paul and Linda (along with Eamonn Andrews) helped to present the 'Big Red Book' to Liverpool boxer John Conteh on TV's "This is Your Life".

On January 9th 1975 the group Wings arrived in New Orleans where they recorded and produced their next studio album "Venus and Mars".

Paul's father Jim McCartney died on March 18th 1976 - R.I.P.

It can certainly be said that however you wish to refer to the world's most famous left-handed bass guitarist, just 'an ex-Beatle' will never do! For in 1977, at the height of Punk Rock and amidst a music chart that claimed the Sex Pistols and The Clash, Paul wrote and issued on November 11th 1977, the best selling single of all time "Mull of Kintyre". "Mull of Kintyre" was to keep that title of best selling single for seven years - and when it was finally outsold by Band Aid's "Do They Know It's Christmas" in 1984, you only had to look at the back sleeve of its successor to find the name Paul McCartney.

On January 16th 1980 the group Wings arrived at Tokyo airport to an already sold-out tour of Japan (January 21st - February 2nd). However, at the airport Paul's luggage was checked by customs and found to contain 219 grams of Marijuana. Immediately Paul was taken to prison and stories of a possible seven year sentence began to fill the world's press. But on January 25th, with the tour already cancelled, Paul was released from jail and deported. It was not surprising that a few weeks later the split of Wings was announced.

On May 16th 1980, a full ten years after its first volume, "McCartney Volume 2" was announced. (Strange that this album, as with the first one, should come immediately after the split up of Paul's group.)

On December 8th 1980 John's death shook the whole world. At the time Paul was working at Air Studio (London) with producer George Martin and was still in a state of shock when commenting to press later that day. Paul's tribute to John "Here Today" (see album "Tug of War") was in the same league as George's "All Those Years Ago" - a real winner which should really have been a single.

To sit down and name all the artists who have worked with Paul would take forever but two artists of note are Stevie Wonder ("Ebony and Ivory") and Michael Jackson ("Say, Say,Say").

The worry about having so much fame (apart from security and privacy) is that the world's press find one an easy target, and they are not always kind. Such as the time when the movie "Give My Regards to Broadstreet" (Paul, Linda, Ringo, Barbara) was issued on November 28th 1984. The press slated it! But in all fairness what they were looking for was a Rock Movie. (Note by Alan Parker: "... I'm sure it will stand the test of time ... besides have you ever bumped into anybody on the street who said it wasn't good ?")

Awards in the McCartney household are nothing new. Although not his style, if he wanted to Paul could cover the walls in his house(s) with Gold Discs and various other musical awards - including 1979's Guinness Book of Records Award for the ONLY-EVER

Rhodium Disc for Achievements in Music.

These awards were further enhanced when on November 28th 1984 Paul McCartney MBE was given yet another honour.In a ceremony at the Picton Library in Liverpool the city's most famous 'son' was granted the Freedom of the City.

Paul's causeworthy efforts also continued, and as a contribution to Glasnost Paul issued "Chobba b CCCP" ("Back in the USSR" again). It was an album of Rock 'n Roll Standards available in Russian only. In the Summer of 1989 all members of Paul's Wings Fan Club received a copy of the album (then changing hands at £100) for FREE! (NB: Fan's wishing to join the Wings Fan Club can write to PO Box 4UP, London, W1A 4UP, England - quote this book.)

With his SEVENTEENTH solo album "Flowers in the Dirt" (including collaboration with Elvis Costello) came the news that Paul would once again be doing some live shows. On June 7th 1989 Fan Club members were given a chance to meet the NEW group (Hamish, Robbie, Chris, Wix and Linda) at a live TV recording for Japanese TV. The tour itself kicked off on September 28th 1989 in Oslo and travelled through Europe and America before finally arriving in England on January 22nd 1990 for sold out shows in Birmingham (NEC) and London (Wembley Arena). At the time of writing the tour is expected to go back to the USA, along with rumoured shows in Japan and the USSR to be announced for 1990; and for those fans who have not seen it,what a show it is! with 2 1/2 hours of laser lighting,explosions and set changes all highlighting numerous hits from the Beatles,Wings and Paul's solo career.

In summing up Paul McCartney,and to quote Alan G. Parker:

".......If you're ever lucky enough to meet 'The Man' there is no star/fan relationship;with Paul it's as though he has known you all his life.He chats about whatever's happening there and then and is always ready to sign for you......

......Thanks for putting the Flowers in the Road!.....

GEORGE HARRISON

("OHNOTHIMAGEN")

The youngest Beatle came into the world on 25th February 1943; born in Liverpool to Harry and Louise Harrison, George belonged to quite a big family.

As with John and the others, music played a large part in George's earlier formative years. At 14 he was a fashionable Teddy Boy and whatever school uniform may have been, George could always be found in a pink shirt, skintight jeans, 'winkle picker' shoes, and a D.A. ('Duck's Arse') hair-do!

Like the others George received a guitar as a present and tried his very best to learn to play it; with his mother Louise at his side, and staying up all hours of the night, George would practise until his fingers bled.

Beatles fans everywhere should thank God that Louise had so much faith in her son (eventually in the other Beatles also) that she would put up with anything!

Although Paul was one year older than George, they met up at school; and as they lived quite near to each other and took the same bus home everyday, it wasn't long before their joint interest in Rock 'n Roll became obvious to everyone.

Once young George discovered that Paul was a member of a group (the Quarrymen) he made it his business to turn up at rehearsals at any given chance. But the group's leader (John Lennon) was 18 years old and tended to see the 15 year old George as just a young kid. It was only when Louise said that she would allow the group to rehearse at her house that Lennon considered young George as a group member - and by the time the name Silver Beatles came along, so did a new lead guitarist called George Harrison.

George's aspirations (as with the others) led him to ploughing all his energies into The Beatles as a group, while simultaneously allowing him to develop his own musical talent and personal aims.

For the next few years George enjoyed the crazy Beatles scene that followed and which is described (along with his personal and family events) in the following chapters. But being the quieter of the Fab Four he tended to be a tremendous thinker; keeping himself to himself. It wasn't too long before he felt that he needed

more out of life ... and out of himself and with this in mind he too began to explore the possibilities of a solo career.

George's solo career actually started on November 1st 1968 with the album "Wonderwall Music", although the album contained only a collection of Indian music and no lyrics. The same could be said for his second solo album "Electronic Sounds" which was released on May 9th 1969 as a collection of just what the title implies.

So it was that on November 30th 1970 that George issued his first conventional solo album, the triple album box set "All Things Must Pass". Despite the high price and size of this package (for in 1970 a triple box set had never been heard of) it still sailed to No. 1 in the Album Charts.

Below are some of the other events that followed in George's life.

November 23rd 1971 - The Indian musician Ravi Shankar had his movie "Raga" premiered in New York - the movie featured George.

June 5th 1972 - At a luncheon given by UNICEF, George and Ravi Shankar were awarded "The Child is The Father of Man" Honour for their concert in Bangladesh (see Chapter 10 - Reunion No. 1).

April 26th 1973 - "The Material World Charitable Foundation Trust" was formed by George.

March 1st 1974 - A USA concert tour for November was announced by George to the world's press.

December 26th 1975 - George appeared on Eric Idle's (Monty Python fame) 'Rutland Weekend TV' Show to sing "The Pirate Song".

April 20th 1976 - George appeared live on stage at the Civic Center USA with the Monty Python Team, singing "The Lumberjack Song".

In spite of his huge fame, George always kept his thoughts to himself. Indeed his own record label Dark Horse (a more fitting name could never be found) went out with the idea of signing other bands but never really did.

Instead the Indian religion of Hari Krishna became a focal point for George in the late Sixties, and at the time of writing many Krishna books still carry George's 1971 Foreword. He eventually became so submerged in the Movement that nothing outside it bothered him so it was no shock to friends and family when he separated from his wife Patti and she went to live with their family friend Eric Clapton (with whom George remained friends).

George and Patti were granted a divorce on June 9th 1977 and Patti married Eric on May 19th 1979.

However George did not wish to dwell on his past and in what seems to be an effort to forget it he teamed up with Eric Idle in 1978 to present the TV movie "The Ruttles - All You Need is Cash" a direct skit on the Beatles in which George took a cameo role.

As regards family, George was the last of the Beatles to become a father. His only child and son, Dhani, was born on August 1st 1978 and on September 2nd 1978 Dhani's mother Olivia Trinidad Arias became the new Mrs. Harrison in a quiet Register Office ceremony.

In 1980 the death of John Lennon had tremendous effect on George who had almost idolised John from the day they met. Indeed it seemed almost fitting that George's next single "All Those Years Ago" (see Chapter 10, Reunion No. 5) was a tribute to John. The strange thing, however, is that when George's autobiography "I, Me, Mine" came along, he never refers to John and almost totally omits The Beatles themselves.

George was by now keeping further and further away from the limelight, and with the release of his November 5th 1982 album "Gone Troppo" George announced that it would be his last album; but was still to surprise people by appearing live on stage with heavy rock group Deep Purple in Sydney on December 14th 1984.

Over the next period of his life, and whilst out of the musical limelight, George filled in a lot of his time as co-producer in his own movie production company called Hand Made Films which was formed on August 1st 1980.

George once said " ... we wanted to call it British Hand Made Films, but before you call something British you must lose a lot of money on it !.

Like all the other Beatles destiny would not let George lie down quietly and by the summer of 1987 rumours were already strong that he would be issuing another album.What followed must of shocked George as much as anyone else-the album"Cloud Nine" was issued and entered the charts in the U.K.top Ten whilst it's lead single"Got My Mind Set On You" topped the U.K.singles chart.

The old magic was still there!

As if that was not enough for his fans,in 1988 George joined the rock super group The Travelling Wilbury's(Bob Dylan,Tom Petty,Jeff Lyne and Roy Orbison R.I.P.).Their album was a huge sucess and at the end of 1989 George was once again very much in the public eye.This prompted him to release"Dark Horse 76-89" (anew compilation album).

For a last word on George we have referred to the inside sleeve of his October 1975 album"Extra Texture"...read all about it!For on the inside sleeve is just ONE WORD- "OHNOTHIMAGEN".("Oh...not...him...again" -for the benefit of foreign readers).

Whilst it was no doubt placed there for a humble joke,to his fans nothing could be further from the truth!

RINGO STARR

(" ... The most famous bit player in Music History ... ")

Born July 7th 1940, Richard ("Ritchie") Starkey (later to become the one and only Ringo Starr) has many memories of his early upbringings in The Dingle - one of the tougher areas of Liverpool - some memories perhaps not quite as happy as others.

When still a young child his parents were divorced. But his mother was soon to remarry; her new husband, Harry Greaves (Richard's stepfather), was to become closer to Ringo than his own father.

Although his earlier schooling was also marred by interruptions due to sickness, he has, in retrospect, been known to say that, despite the sickness, there isn't a single part of his life that he would change ...

Because of his fascination for wearing a ring on almost every finger, young Ritchie soon got the nickname "Ringo" from his school chums but it was not till later that he would add "Starr" to his name.

Whilst at school and at the tender age of fifteen, Ringo acquired his first drum kit and while the Silver Beatles were whipping up a storm in Liverpool, Ritchie was drummer of Rory Storm and the Hurricanes - one of The Beatles' chief competitors on the growing Merseybeat circuit. But he was still undecided about his future - so much so that when Ringo went with The Hurricanes to Butlins Holiday Camp in North Wales for the Summer Season of 1962, he had already decided to give up music and get an apprenticeship as soon as the season was over. This was despite the fact that it was at Butlins where he added "Starr" to his nickname having taken it from the camp's night time cabaret "Starr Time".

However it was during that same summer that King-size Taylor and The Dominoes asked Ringo to become their drummer but before he had time to think about an answer he was contacted by Brian Epstein to become drummer with Brian's latest signing - a group known as The Beatles. With The Beatles already having a recording contract Brian's offer was obviously the more attractive and even before finishing his season with The Hurricanes Ringo left to join The Beatles.

What follows, and indeed covers the numerous events surrounding both the musical career and personal family life of Ringo during the years 1962 to 1970, will unfold in the forthcoming chapters of the book you are about to read and so it is now that we travel forward to March 27th 1970 and the issuing of Ringo's first solo album "Sentimental Journey" which became Ringo's first tentative step into the world of his own solo career - the record, like its title may suggest, was merely a collection of old Cover versions of songs which his mother and stepfather had loved.

The following facts give a brief insight into Ringo's solo career and hopefully whet the reader's appetite for "In The Lap Of The Gods And and The Hands Of The Beatles - Volume Two - The Solo Years" (currently under production).

On May 9th 1970 Ringo and Maureen were guests of honour at the Cannes Film Festival for the screening of "Woodstock", the movie of the event.

Ringo began recording his second solo album "Beaucoups of The Blues" in Nashville (USA) on June 22nd 1970; eight days later it was complete.

On April 25th 1971 Ringo made a guest appearance on Cilla Black's BBC TV show "Cilla". The pair sang a duet of the old Beatles' number "Act Naturally".

September 3rd 1971 - Ringo joined forces with designer Robin Cruickshank to form the company Ringo Or Robin Ltd for the purpose of furniture design - a two week exhibition of the pair's designs was opened on September 13th at Liberty's Department Store, New York.

September 27th 1972 - In a bizarre suicide pact with his mother at their Liverpool home "Stormsville", Rory Storm (of Hurricanes fame) is found dead - Rory could never come to terms with the fact that The Beatles found world fame whilst he did not.

On July 6th 1973 Ringo and Maureen attended the London farewell party of David Bowie after his 'last ever' gig - with hindsight we now know this 'last gig' was not to be the case.

February 6th 1974 - BBC Radio One's "My Top Twelve" show featured Ringo Starr. The records he chose were rather strange to say the least - omitting any possibilities of playing a single Beatles record!

October 10th 1975 and Ken Russell's controversial story of the composer

Franz Liszt strangely titles "Lisztomania" opened in New York. Stranger still was the role taken by Ringo Starr - that of the Pope.

On May 19th 1980 Ringo and Barbara Bach (now married) were in a car crash just outside London. Although the car was a write off the couple were hospitalised for a few days but suffered only shock.

On December 9th of the same year Ringo and Barbara arrived at the Dakota Building, New York, to comfort Yoko Ono following John Lennon's tragic death. In what cannot have been a good time for any of the group it's worth pointing out that over a short period Ringo had not only lost John, but also Marc Bolan (T-Rex) on September 16th 1977 and Keith Moon (The Who) on September 7th 1978, both of whom he was extremely close.

On the face of things Ringo has been described as everything from the 'Gentleman Beatle' (New York Times) to 'Everybody's favourite Uncle' (as he was described by Paul McCartney). As history quite plainly shows, a drummer's lot is not usually a happy one for in most cases when a major group disbands the drummer fades into obscurity. This could never be said of Richard Starkey MBE!

An acting career had opened up to Ringo before The Beatles had even called it a day; and with successes like "Magic Christian" and "That'll Be The Day" under his belt there was no shortage of acting offers.

His marriage to Maureen was, it seems, destined to fail and on July 17th 1975 Ringo and Maureen were granted a divorce. Although she received a high cash settlement and has since remarried, she has always claimed there will be space in her heart for Ringo.

However, the marriage was indeed fruitful having produced three children.

Zak, the eldest, was born in the shadow of Beatlemania. It was not surprising then that Zak went into a musical career. Always close to his father, he has become an internationally recognised session drummer - having worked with John Entwistle (The Who) and Adrian Smith (Iron Maiden), and toured with The Icicle Works (a successful Liverpool band).

Zak was married on January 22nd 1985 to Sarah Menkides in a secret London ceremony (so secret in fact that Ringo was told the next day). Sarah gave birth to their daughter Tatia Jayne on September 7th of the same year.

Ringo, the first Beatle grandfather, was over the moon and said to one press reporter "... George (Harrison) sent me some flowers - as if it was something I'd done ...!"

Jason, Ringo's second son was born one month after "Sgt. Pepper". Despite the publicity surrounding The Beatles and their families at that time, he has remained in the background and after his parents split spent the largest amount of time with his mother.

Lee, Ringo's only daughter, is a 'Daddy's Girl' in every sense of the word, having been evident at numerous showbusiness parties and movie premieres with her father. She has never had any musical ambitions which once prompted her father to say:

"... well, two drummers is enough in any family ...!"

It was during the filming of the comedy "Caveman" in February 1980 that Ringo met ex-Bond girl Barbara Bach (herself divorced with children). It has been said by cast and crew alike that love blossomed overnight.

The pair were to be seen together frequently at various parties and functions and it was no shock when in April 1980 they were married. Their home was to be Tittenhurst Park, a property Ringo bought from John (Lennon) back in 1973.

Always a hit with younger people, Ringo was asked to narrate an animated children's television show based on Reverend W. Awdry's "Thomas The Tank Engine". From its pilot episode on October 9th 1984 the programme became highly successful, still running even now after its one initial series. By the time an American version "Shining Time Station" was made, Ringo and the series were so compatible that rather than just narrating the show, he played the Stationmaster.

Although "Thomas The Tank Engine" was a considerable success it was no secret that Ringo's musical career was on the slide, with his last album "Old Wave" only finding a contract for release in Germany. In spite of attempts by EMI at CD compilations of earlier chart successes (e.g. "Photograph", etc.) Ringo, without Paul, George or John behind him, seemed to have little joy in the recording field.

In the summer of 1989 the British press got hold of the story that Ringo and

Barbara had checked into Betty Ford's Alcoholic Rehabilitation Center in the USA. According to the story Ringo was then consuming upto one and a half bottles of brandy per day. After a few weeks in the Center the pair were discharged but rumours in the world press became rife. Ringo was said to be replacing his old friend Keith Moon as the drummer on The Who's 25th Anniversary World Tour (although when the event finally happened Simon Philips, son of the late bandleader Sid Philips, played the drums). But in reality Ringo HAD found himself a drumming job - on the comeback album of his old friend George Harrison under the title "Cloud Nine".

We are not sure if it was the "Cloud Nine" album or Ringo's guest stage appearance with Bob Dylan in the USA that brought him back to his old self. In the short space of time that followed Ringo had (with help from Rhino Records, USA) put together "Starr Struck Volume Two" - a collection of his own material from 1973-1981. (The title "Volume Two" was strange insofar as there has never been a "Volume One".)

Within days of this album's release word was already out that Ringo was rehearsing with a new touring band including Billy Preston, Nills Lofgren, Joe Walsh and others. So it was not surprising when, in September of 1989, Pepsi-Cola announced the "Ringo and his All-Starr Band USA Tour".

So successful was this handful of American shows (probably because of the inclusion of a number of Beatles' songs including "Yellow Submarine") that when the tour came to an end Ringo announced plans for European and even UK concert performances. At the time of writing he is currently undergoing a highly successful Christmas/New Year tour of Japan.

Having put his problems with alcohol behind him and having gained a much respected album in "Starr Struck", Ringo's future now looks so bright that it is no wonder 'shades' seem to have become a permanent fixture on the face of the 'Gentleman Beatle'.

CHAPTER ONE

"NO MORE PLAYING IN SMALL CLUBS FOR EIGHT HOURS"

The Cast are born:

February 18th 1933 Yoko Ono Tokyo Japan
September 19th 1934 Brian Epstein Liverpool England
September 10th 1939 Cynthia Powell Blackpool England
June 23rd 1940 Stuart Sutcliffe Edinburgh Scotland
July 7th 1940 Richard Starkey Liverpool England
October 9th 1940 John Winston Lennon Liverpool England
September 24th 1941 Linda Eastman New York USA
November 24th 1941 Randolph Peter Best Madras India
June 18th 1942 James Paul McCartney Liverpool England
February 25th 1943 George Harrison Liverpool England
March 17th 1945 Patricia Anne Boyd London England
April 5th 1946 Jane Asher London England
4th August 1946 Maureen Cox Liverpool England

Whichever way one looks at it they hardly had too much to shout about since they met on June 15th 1957, but for two fresh youngsters from Liverpool no one could have predicted the future that was in store for them. John Lennon and Paul McCartney were here.

What had gone was fairly predictable for a local beat group in the late 50's - the odd gig, a few rehearsals, many line-up changes, and even a rough record booth version of "That'll Be The Day" backed with "In Spite of All the Danger" (the first ever Lennon-McCartney number committed to vinyl - which was destined to be far from the last).

The first of January 1962 was by no means a nice day. The snow fell from the heavens interminably, as if it was determined to cover the whole of England (including Merseyside) before noon. But the weather alone could not dampen the spirits of the four piece band from Liverpool preparing for their trip to London, a long hard drive ahead of them. For John Lennon, Paul McCartney, George Harrison and Pete Best this was to be one of the most important days of their lives - the day The Beatles auditioned for Decca Records.

Mersey Beat was a rock 'n roll newspaper which was printed, edited and issued from Liverpool by a young Bill Harry - an art college friend of John Lennon. The magazine was Harry's own way of letting people know what was going on in the growing Liverpool beat scene.

Indeed, it was partly through this publication that The Beatles had met Mr. Brian Epstein, the manager of NEMS Music Store, and it was Brian who had worked out the deal that sent them to Decca for the audition of January 1st.

On January 4th 1962 Mersey Beat readers voted The Beatles their Favourite Group.

The group had for the most part of their brief career left all bookings and last words on other business to Allan Williams, a small-time Club owner who made side money by sending groups to Hamburg - but for one reason or another they had never signed with Williams. Hell! They'd never signed with ANYBODY - not until January 24th when they signed an official contract with NEMS Enterprises Ltd., a firm owned by Brian Epstein.

Like all good local bands the group had begun to pick up a large home-town following - so much so that they had become 'stars' at home with their own incredible amount of fan mail. The mail, as with the interest in the group, grew bigger and on February 1st 1962 Freda Kelly became President of the Official Beatles Fan Club.

By March of the same year, the group were awaiting news from London about their audition with Decca. Brian decided to take a trip himself to the Big City. On arrival he met with Dick Rowe from Decca who turned him down saying ... "Guitar Bands like The Shadows were on their way out."

Undeterred by Rowe's comments, Brian took the tapes to other record labels that same day, including Columbia, HMV and EMI - but again was unsuccessful with them all.

When Brian arrived back in Liverpool, with the bad news, morale in the group sank to an all-time low. Something was needed to boost the morale, to weather the storm. Brian's thoughts materialised in the form of a seven week stint at the Star-Club in Hamburg, West Germany. It was April 5th.

Stuart Sutcliffe was Liverpool's most promising art student and his rebel image endeared him to the other college students. That is where he became first a friend and later a flatmate of John Lennon. So tightly bound was John's friendship with Stu in their earlier days that after the latter won an Art Contest and bought a guitar, John let him join the group (then called The Quarrymen) even though Stu couldn't play a note. In fact at any gigs that Sutcliffe ever did with the group he always stood with his back to the audience.

However, as time went on and the group got better, Stu decided to leave the group and settle down in Hamburg with Astrid, his German fiancee, whom he had met on one of the group's earlier visits to Hamburg. Unfortunately, just after the group arrived in Germany for their seven week stint from Brian, Stuart died suddenly of a brain haemorrhage resulting from having been jumped by a gang of Liverpool 'toughs' some years earlier.

Brian and Mrs. Sutcliffe flew out to Germany to return Stu's body for a simple funeral in Liverpool. He was 21.

After arriving back in England, Brian decided to give the tapes from Decca another try in the hope that he would be able to give 'the Lads' some good news on their return from Hamburg. He left again for London.

This time Epstein played the tapes to music publisher Syd Coleman who in turn introduced Brian to producer George Martin. Now if Brian Epstein had seemed a strange choice for Manager, George Martin was 'out of this world' for a Rock 'n Roll producer.

Martin had undergone full classical training and had spent the last few years producing 'Comedy' records at Parlophone - a small label owned by EMI. Brian told George that "... one day they will be bigger than Elvis." George must have liked something that he'd heard and concluded the meeting by telling Brian that he'd give the Lads a try.

Knowing that Bill Harry trusted him enough to print a story on his word, Brian rang him and told him that The Beatles had signed with Parlophone Records. At this point the story was only half true, inasmuch as George Martin still had to convince his bosses. But what the hell!

On June 4th, The Beatles once again headed for the Big City. This time for their audition with Parlophone.

Because of both Stu's death and earlier record label rejection morale in the

group was not at its highest. This wasn't helped by the fact that by the end of the day George Martin told Brian that the group had one weak link - that of drummer Pete Best.

Brian talked George's worries over with John, Paul and George. Much to Brian's dismay they had been thinking the same way. They had decided that they would like him replaced with Richard Starkey, a drummer with local group Rory Storm and the Hurricanes, who had helped the group out when Pete was ill. Richard was now calling himself "Ringo Starr" on account of his many rings, and the group he was with were playing in a spot called "Starr Time" at Butlins.

After much deliberation, and the fact that the ever cagey Lennon didn't think that it was anybody's place in the group to tell Pete but Brian, Pete's fate had been decided.

August 16th 1977 was to become one of the blackest days in Rock 'n Roll history with the death of a legend. Elvis Presley, Rock's officially appointed 'King', had died at the age of 42.

However, for Randolph Peter Best August 16th 1962 couldn't have been much blacker - it was the day he was summoned to NEMS' offices to see Brian. His boss had asked to see him - probably a change in a club date, news from Parlophone, who knows! He didn't really know. But whatever was going on in his mind couldn't possibly have cushioned him for what was to come.

Brian looked a little nervous when Pete arrived. He skated round the subject for a short time before coming out with it and telling Pete the bad news - it was a bombshell! The group had a good chance of going somewhere at last - and he was out!

To make matters worse, "Mersey Beat" carried the story "Pete Best Sacked" on what could only be described as a crazily happy day in the lives of the others. For on August 23rd '62 John married Cynthia Powell at Mount Pleasant Register Office.

Pete Best was the most good-looking of the group and as such attracted the lion's share of the fan mail from their Liverpool followers. At that stage The Beatles hadn't thought out their first non-Pete gig. Taking place at the Cavern in Liverpool on August 27th, it went quite smoothly but also very productively - with George Harrison receiving a black eye in a scuffle.But it wasn't too long before the fans got used to Ringo - after all who couldn't like Ringo!

Parlophone liked what they heard; so much so that on September 4th The Beatles were invited down to EMI's Abbey Road Studio No. 2 to make a single. When they got there George Martin had hired a session drummer, Andy White, because no one had told him about Ringo. All the same, TWO versions of "Love Me Do" were recorded, one with Ringo and the other with Andy.

Whilst in London, the group were photographed by professional Dezzo Hoffman. George's black eye makes these earlier photos pretty easy to recognise.

Even though the group had signed with NEMS, there was no official contract between them and Brian. On October 1st that was changed. Brian had a five year contract drawn up as their Manager which he, Ringo and John signed. Paul and George had to be signed for by their respective fathers as they were still legally minors.

October 5th saw the release of Parlophone Records PR4949 "Love Me Do" backed with "PS I Love You". The Beatles' first single was out.

Brian wanted to take no chances and he ordered numerous advance copies for NEMS Music Stores. In addition he booked the group into Dawson's Music (Widnes) for a 'Meet the Fans' signing session - after all a good push was all it needed!

"Love Me Do" peaked at Number 27. A good move for their first attempt but not good enough for Parlophone to have faith in another Lennon-McCartney number. However they came up with "How Do You Do It" for the group to record. Not wanting to 'rock the boat' they agreed to record "How Do You Do It" but also asked George to let them record "Please, Please Me". George didn't see the point as they had played it at their audition and it was a slow, drab number. But as John and Paul said that they had revamped it, George agreed to give it a try.

"As soon as I heard the new version I knew it was a Number One" said Martin.Strangely enough, "How Do You Do It" was passed on to Gerry and the Pacemakers and also became a Number One. December 17th 1962 saw the dawning of another first in the group's career. Granada Television went to the Cavern to film The Beatles for its "People and Places" TV slot. It went out live and earned the group the princely sum of thirty five pounds for their performance.

Beatlemania was about to begin.

CHAPTER TWO

"BEATLEMANIA"

It's been said over the years that memories fade and facts, like other stories, are passed on - a little added, some taken away. In the Sixties drugs had become a new 'experience' and it was once said by ex-Monkee Peter Tork that "... anybody who can remember it as it was day by day either wasn't there or they were lying." So from this point we move on with that quote in mind.

Fresh back from Hamburg and still quite run-down from the trip, the group set off for a five day tour of Scotland. But it was only on their return to Liverpool that the first sign of 'things to come' took place.

The group played the Majestic Ballroom, Birkenhead. Not only was the show sold out but 500 ticketless fans were turned away.

In late January Brian decided that although his 'Boys' were getting good exposure in the UK and Germany, the big USA market knew nothing of The Beatles. So he signed a deal with Jay-Vee Records to issue Beatles records in America.

A few days later on February 2nd, some three months on the tail of their local TV debut on "People and Places", the group were zoomed into every sitting room in England on TV's "Thank Your Lucky Stars".

Parlophone were now eager to get an Album from the group, but it had to be fast, after all they might only last a few more months. So on February 11th studio time was booked and in one mammoth 12-hour recording session "Please, Please Me" the album was recorded. So keen were the group that,that day five other songs were also laid down in addition to what was needed.

More good news for the group came on February 16th when "Please, Please Me" became The Beatles' first Number One single.

But even with all that was happening, Jay Livingstone, the then head of Capitol Records (USA), who were owned by EMI, informed George Martin that he would not be issuing any Beatles records at that time because he felt they didn't suit the American market.

Meanwhile at home in the UK The Beatles were fast proving that they did suit

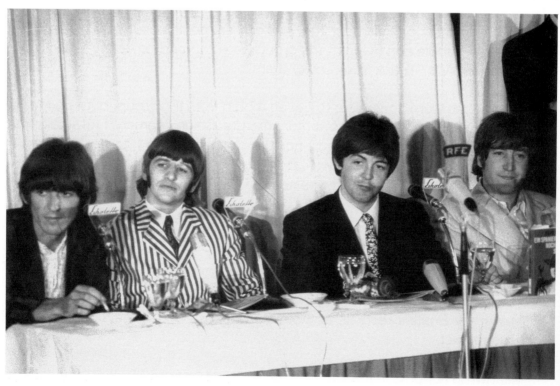

'the market'. Helen Shapiro, booked to top the bill on a Manchester show to be seen live on TV, was moved to second on the bill because The Beatles were considered to be more popular and had to go on last.

Forseeing the group's potential, Brian decided that they should have their own publishing company so as to ensure a larger cut for themselves from their own work. As a result Northern Songs Ltd. was born on February 24th with Messrs Lennon, McCartney, Epstein and Dick James as Directors.

The Beatles' fame continued to grow and later in the year the New Musical Express published its Annual Poll results. In a ceremony at the Empire Pool, Wembley, The Beatles were awarded "The Most Promising Act of 1962."

On April 8th Cynthia gave birth to John Charles Julian Lennon - later to become a star in his own right and to be featured as the subject of "Hey Jude", one of The Beatles' greatest later hits.

By this time the group were constantly being bothered by the press and Brian appointed Tony Barrow as the official Beatles Press Agent to cover all press/public relation. It was this concern with 'image' that led Brian into changing the appearance of the group when he first took them over. He now felt that a more formal change was needed that would hopefully start some kind of fashion cult within the fans.

The now famous grey collar-less stage suits and cuban-heelboots had arrived!

By the middle of the year more and more people in the business wanted their chance to present the group in their own way. So, on June 14th, the BBC announced a fifteen week radio series to be called "Pop Go The Beatles" and to be presented live each week from Broadcasting House. The Beatles were on their way!

Paul was the first of The Beatles to celebrate his 21st birthday as, during earlier days, John and Ringo had already passed that special age. Brian decided that Paul's party should be a somewhat special and very up-market affair.

Various other EMI recording stars including Cliff Richard and The Shadows were invited to the party, which was held in Paul's Aunt Jinny's back garden at Birkenhead. Earlier that day Paul was given the traditional 'bumps' for the press by John, George and Ringo outside EMI in Manchester Square.

On a happier note, 'Beatlemania' became more visible on July 21st when in

Blackpool 4,000 ticketless fans were turned away from the Queens Theatre just before the start of the group's concert and stood outside all through the show.

The first of August saw the publication of Beatles Monthly in which issue No. 1 was run as a kind of extended newsletter in conjunction with the Fan Club. Consequently the group gave exclusive magazine photo and interview sessions. So large was The Beatles' popularity that in 1989, twenty six years later, there would still be a Beatles Monthly.

As if their outstanding successes weren't enough, the group's next single "She Loves You" saw an incredible 500,000 orders in ADVANCE - making it a Number One BEFORE its release. More good news was to follow when trade magazine Record Retailer announced that such were the sales of "She Loves You" that no other record could possibly knock it from the top spot for at least four weeks.

This was fabulous news for the fans - not least for a young girl working at the Cavern cloakroom that September. With help from Brian and Ringo (who first spotted her) a young lady called Priscilla White was given a name change and sent to fulfil her wish to become a singer. As Cilla Black she was later to become a household name in Britain.

The schedule for the remainder of the year was starting to gather momentum and getting fairly heavy. As a 'breather', Brian suggested that everyone should take a three week vacation. Not wanting to argue with their boss, it wasn't long before Paul and Ringo were flying to Athens, John and Cyn were on their way to holiday with Astrid and George flew to America with brother Peter to visit their sister.

By the time the group returned from their various vacations, Brian had bought himself a house in London which he felt was the best place to be based. Paul followed suit by moving in with actress and girlfriend Jane Asher AND her parents, while John, George and Ringo each bought their own place just outside the city.

On October 11th, The Beatles received their first Gold Disc for selling over one million copies of "She Loves You" while at the press conference it was announced officially (some twelve months after the event) that John was married and was indeed a father. So much for surprises!

Only two days later, on October 13th, the group were asked to 'Top the Bill' on TV's much acclaimed "Sunday Night At The London Palladium". They went down so well that the following day 'Beatlemania' was well and truly born when the world's press used the word to describe the events of the TV show.

Later that week the group recorded a special Christmas message to be pressed as a flexi disc and given away to all their Fan Club Members later in the year. The first time this was done it was a one-off but the gift was so well received and was capable of being made so easily within a small time frame that the group decided to repeat the process every year until 1970.

Following their success at the London Palladium the group had started to climb the 'social ladder' - although none of them would admit to it, and on November 4th appeared on the "Royal Variety Show". Their short set was ended by another easy way to win over fans and press alike as John made the now famous comment:

"For our next number we'd like to ask your help. Would the people in the cheaper seats clap and the rest of you just rattle your jewels ... " On that last number they received a standing ovation.

It is understood, however, that Brian had to be revived backstage with smelling salts after having been in total dread of what John was originally going to say following comments in the car on the way down to London. (The Author feels it would be better for all concerned if those somewhat 'private' comments remained so in the interests of all concerned.)

News of The Beatles was now beginning to spread internationally and on November 10th a Dutch Fan Club was formed, thus making a Fan Club in almost every country of the world except Russia. Fans in Russia were not to be allowed a Fan Club by the State until 1987 - almost twenty five years later!

Later in November EMI Chief Sir Joseph Lockwood decided to present the group with his own special Award for Achievement in 1962 and 1963. As a kind of 'thank you' to their fans for 2 great years the group did a special FREE gig for their fans at the Wimbledon Palais in early December. All 3,000 fans present got to meet a Beatle and went home with an autograph. Most Members even took along their "Beatles Christmas Record" which they were given free by the Club some days earlier.

With Christmas closing in and the mood becoming more festive, Christmas Eve saw the opening night of "The Beatles Christmas Show" at the Astoria Theatre, London (which was to run until early January 1964). After the Christmas Eve show, Brian chartered a helicopter to get the group back to Liverpool in time for Christmas with their families.

CHAPTER THREE

"FOUR FRENZIED LITTLE LORD FAUNTLEROYS EARNING £1000 A WEEK"

1964 was the year when it was finally realised that there was no turning back. What England already knew became world knowledge, and if 1963 was hard - well, to quote Cynthia Lennon, 1964 was "... like being in the eye of a hurricane ..."

Capitol Records started off the year by deciding that they could no longer ignore The Beatles. Consequently, on January 1st a giant (at that time) $50,000 campaign was launched to promote the group in the USA. During the same week "I Wanna Hold Your Hand" was issued as the group's first US single.

The group themselves left the UK for Paris on January 14th - all except for Ringo who was stranded in fog-bound Liverpool. He was to fly out and join the rest the next day.

By now the group had such a following in Germany that two of their songs were re-recorded by themselves IN GERMAN. On January 29th "Sie Liebt Dich" ("She Loves You") was released in Germany. Not surprisingly it became the UK's best selling import.

In early February the group were ready to set out on their first US tour. What followed was altogether totally unpredictable.

When the group arrived in the USA the crowds were so big that they assumed somebody big, perhaps the President, was due to land at the same time. It was only when they stepped off the plane however, that the screams and fans were all theirs. Indeed, on the day The Beatles first set foot on US soil, they were the USA's Number One Band.

As if musical success wasn't enough they continued to break records of all kinds. On George's 21st birthday, for example, if there was such a record for the largest number of Birthday Cards received, try this for size ... a total of SIXTY postal sacks delivered some 30,000 Birthday Cards from all over the world.

By this time, everybody wanted to make some money from The Beatles. Polydor Records bought the rights and then released the 1960 (German Release Only)

album entitled "Tony Sheridan and the Beat Brothers". Yes, it was a winner, and yes, the Beat Brothers were of course The Beatles.

In late March John Lennon's first book called "In His Own Write" was published. It is a mishmash of John's strange 'play-on-words' style and is illustrated by weird cartoons of cripples and strange animals. The book sold over 400,000 copies worldwide.

During the same period American television crews travelled to Liverpool to interview Pete Best, the group's ex-drummer, about his days with the group. On way or another, anyone with a contact could be a star!

Another Beatles 'first' came in the USA on March 31st when musical history was made. All the 5 top singles were Beatles records and a further seven singles in the Top 50 belonged to the group.

By this time Brian Epstein had decided that with The Beatles he really did have too much work for himself alone and in early April he appointed Derek Taylor (former Daily Express reporter) as his Personal Assistant.

Later that month the English Literary Society (possibly because of sales) presented John with a Special Award for "In His Own Write" at their Annual Dinner in London's Dorchester Hotel. John was so nervous about being amongst such great writers his speech was simply - "Thanks very much - you've got a nice face."

Beatlemania was now in its heyday, but, as with any adulation, the price of fame was beginning to take its toll. The first sign came on June 3rd when Ringo was admitted to hospital suffering from exhaustion.

As it was just prior to a Beatles tour of Europe, the Far East and Austrailia and knowing that dates could not be cancelled, Brian replaced Ringo temporarily with Jimmy Nicol, a London session drummer.

A few days later, because of their heavy schedule and the fact that John had spent very little time with his family, Brian flew Cynthia, Julian and Aunt Mimi out to Hong Kong to join the group.

Ringo was discharged from hospital on June 11th and with Jimmy Nicol playing his last gig with the group on June 13th over in Adelaide (Australia), Ringo rejoined the group in Melbourne on June 15th. The Beatles were back together.

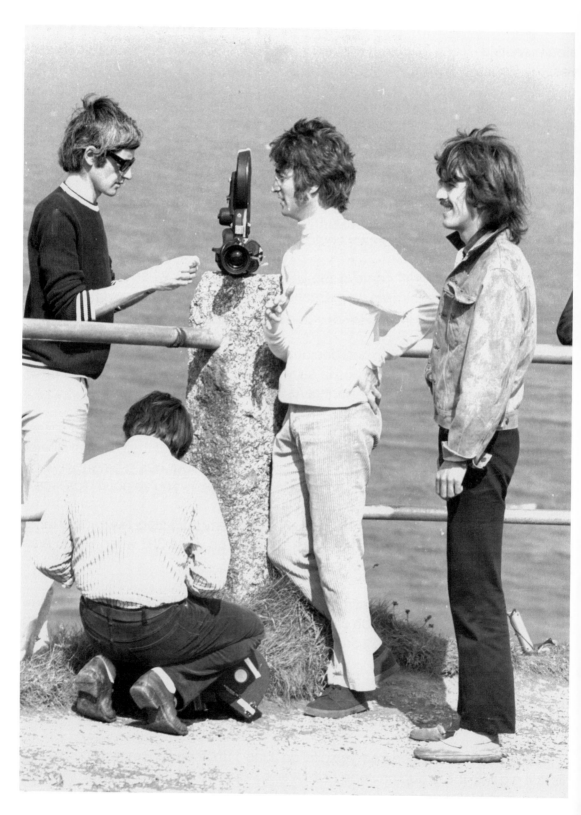

Later that month Ringo went into hospital again, this time to part company with his tonsils! Unfortunately the hospital in question could not be kept a secret from the fans and its switchboard was jammed with people wanting to know how he was. In fact there were so many "How's Ringo?"'s that the G.P.O. set up a special "Ringo Line".

In early July, Decca Records (possibly wanting to make up for the biggest cock-up of all time in turning down The Beatles) issued a single "I'm Gonna Knock On Your Door" by The Pete Best Four. It was quite predictable no big hit.

In contrast, July 6th saw the Royal Premiere at the Pavilion Cinema London of the group's first movie "A Hard Day's Night" with Brian and all the group in attendance. The film, which was in black and white, started shooting in March '64 and featured a role by Wilfrid Bramble (very popular in the British comedy "Steptoe and Son") as Paul's Grandfather. Its subject was a day in the life of the group and yes, it was a hit!

Wealth was now very much a part of the phenomenal fame which The Beatles enjoyed and Paul, having proved that fame does bring riches by buying his father a £1,200 birthday present in the shape of "Drake's Drum", a race horse, set the pace for a spending spree by the others.

On the day following the movie premiere Ringo celebrated his 24th birthday by receiving a pair of solid gold and diamond cuff links from Brian.

During the next two weeks both John and George bought large new houses. John was first on July 9th with a home in Weybridge for which he paid £20,000. George spent the same amount on July 17th for a house in Esher.

George had also been writing songs, two of which managed to find themselves onto each album. But as his songs had not come under the banner of Northern Songs for publishing, George formed his own company, Harrisongs Ltd., on September 11th.

The spending spree continued when, on Brian's birthday on September 19th, the group took two days off work to celebrate with their boss and buy him an antique telephone worth £18,000; after all, what else would one buy an antique collecting boss who had put them 'at the top.'

Early October saw the publication of "A Cellar-full of Noise", Brian's autobiography, which was mainly ghost written by Derek Taylor who received £600 on publication and 20% of all sales worldwide. Everyone was riding the 'gravy train', and the ride didn't look like coming to an end.

At the Ivor Novello Awards in London on October 25th, the group walked away with not one but FIVE awards! (Author's note - if any readers are counting the number of Beatles 'firsts' during their career, I should stop now - you'll only lose track.)

Paul's mother had died on October 31st 1956, long before her son had shot to fame; even though everyone cherished her memory, they couldn't have been happier when, on November 24th, Paul's father re-married, his bride to be was Angela (Mrs. Jim McCartney).

What a year! and the Festive Season was again just around the corner.

On December 5th Freda Kelly (UK Fan Club President) told the world in a magazine interview that there were then some 65,000 current UK members. (Authors note - if anyone can help we would like to track down Ms. Freda Kelly, wherever she may be, for current day comment.)

With Christmas upon them, George decided to leave for the Bahamas on December 18th. With him was top model Patti Boyd with whom he had been close friends since they met on the set of "A Hard Day's Night".

Meanwhile back at home Boxing Day saw 'The Fab Four' placed on display in wax both at Madame Tussaud's London and Blackpool Exhibitions at the same time as Neil Aspinall (Road Crew Chief) was receiving a belated Christmas present from his 'four bosses' - a Jaguar sports car!

Fame and Riches DID go together - at least for some!

CHAPTER FOUR

"WITH THIS SORT OF POWER WE CAN DO ANYTHING"

By 1965 The Beatles were indeed at the top of their hectic profession. As George Martin once put it - "at Abbey Road Studio we had a licence to kill." No one knew how long it would last but it certainly didn't appear to be winding down within the near future. Where records were concerned, '65 would see the breaking of yet more. It was, in terms of glory, THEIR year.

John kicked off the year by showing once again that he had a 'goon-like' sense of humour. He was 'tops' with the fans when he made a guest appearance on the BBC Radio comedy show "Not Only But Also" (later to be followed by a TV show of the same name).

In late January John and Cynthia went to St. Moritz for a holiday with George and Judy Martin. While they were away a Cynthia Lennon Fan Club was set up totally independently.

By this time Ringo was also feeling the attractions of a family life and on February 11th married his long time girlfriend Maureen Cox, a Liverpool based hairdresser. Although Paul was away in Africa, John and George were at the ceremony with Brian as the Best Man.

As for business, their music was achieving the same phenomenal success as its creators, and on February 18th Northern Songs Ltd. announced that it wished to go public. Not only did shares sell very well but also The Times newspaper was soon referring to the shares as "like gold dust".

The press, however, were not always as complimentary and in April stories began to appear in the nationals that Brian was in financial difficulties. The funny thing was that, almost as if to snub the reports, Brian bought the Saville Theatre in London. As if looking for alternative 'sensationalism', the next press story was that Pete Best was working as a baker in Liverpool - no one took any notice.

It was at this point that Paul decided that life within the same house as his girlfriend's parents was not beneficial long term, and so, on April 14th, he paid £40,000 for a large Victorian townhouse in Cavendish Avenue - just around the corner from the Abbey Road Studios. On the same day he sent a telegram to the

CND (Campaign for Nuclear Disarmament) saying that he was in full support of their work.

But by June the wheels of business were well and truly back in motion and Brian (via Northern Songs) issued a press statement that to date 1,337 Cover Versions of Lennon and McCartney songs were available on vinyl.

As early as June 12th stories had been rumoured and were later confirmed that the group were soon to receive the MBE (Member of the British Empire medal) for their outstanding contribution to music. John's comment was - "I thought you had to fight wars, not make records." Indeed those who HAD fought in the Great Wars felt the same way, and on June 14th five old soldiers returned their own hard-earned medals to the Queen in protest. This was followed by more old soldiers doing the same, in further protest, on June 18th.

Books and music were still The Beatles prime concern and on June 24th John's satirical novel "Spaniard in the Works" was released. Like its predecessor it was also an instant success with the fans. This was to be closely followed by a Royal Premiere of the group's second movie "Help" on July 29th. In contrast to their first movie, this second was in colour and was attended by Princess Margaret and Lord Snowdon. They were both joined in the Royal Box by the UK's other current 'royalty' - Messrs Lennon, McCartney, Harrison and Starr.

In the run up to the Premiere, Ringo followed John and George's almost 12 month example and on July 24th paid £37,000 for a new home in the stockbroker belt at Weybridge. The house purchase fever continued even further when on August 7th John bought a seaside cottage in Bournemouth which he gave to his Aunt Mimi as her new home.

Musically, The Beatles were now worldwide 'mega stars' and were respected by both the general public and other stars alike; both for their talent and their business acumen. This was exemplified the day after the Premiere of "Help", and at the request of John and George, when Suba Films (a company owned by Brian) filmed a live concert by The Who and The Animals.

Ever the cautious businessman, Brian made another of those moves which in turn made other rock managers sit up. On August 12th he took out a one million pound insurance policy on The Beatles.

The day after, the group flew out to New York to meet another of the long list of stars who were crying out to meet them - Bob Dylan. It was a meeting which was to result in great musical impact on both sides over the next few years.

Whilst out in the USA the group attended a party with the famous 'in crowd' of the USA. At this party it was rumoured that Peter and Jane Fonda may have introduced the group to LSD - a mind altering chemical. The substance has the capability of sending the subject on a 'trip'. John had such a good time at the party that afterward he wrote a song about his experiences on LSD. The song was called "She Said She Said."

What happened next to the group has been exaggerated, lied about and even written off by many books over the years since then. But on August 27th The Beatles did in fact to go to 'Gracelands' to meet the greatest Rock n' Roll 'King' of all time - Elvis Presley! It was to be their only meeting.

They stayed for three hours, chatted and played Monopoly (with REAL money). But what is up for most dispute is that they were reported to have had a 'jam' session as well. If that DID happen, it's likely that the only other person to know about it would be Colonel Tom Parker - Elvis's life long manager. It is also probable that if the event did indeed take place, Colonel Parker would no doubt have taped the session. As yet no tapes have ever come to light - let's just say we will wait!

On September 20th ex-group member Pete Best tried his recording luck again with a USA-only release of "Boys" (a song now often sung 'live' by Ringo). The single flopped.

Their fame in the USA continued when on September 25th the world (via USA of course) was given its first view of a new Beatles Cartoon TV Show. No need to worry about the 'ratings' - it was a hit!

It was now time to return to the UK.

Back in the UK the memorable day of October 26th arrived - it was the day that The Beatles were to go to Buckingham Palace to be presented with their MBE's. While at the Palace, the group signed albums for Prince Charles and Princess Anne and, it is rumoured, smoked 'pot' in the Palace toilets.

The group's power of fame was once again demonstrated on November 25th when Harrods (London's most famous store) was closed to the public for 2 hours whilst Brian and the group did their Christmas shopping.

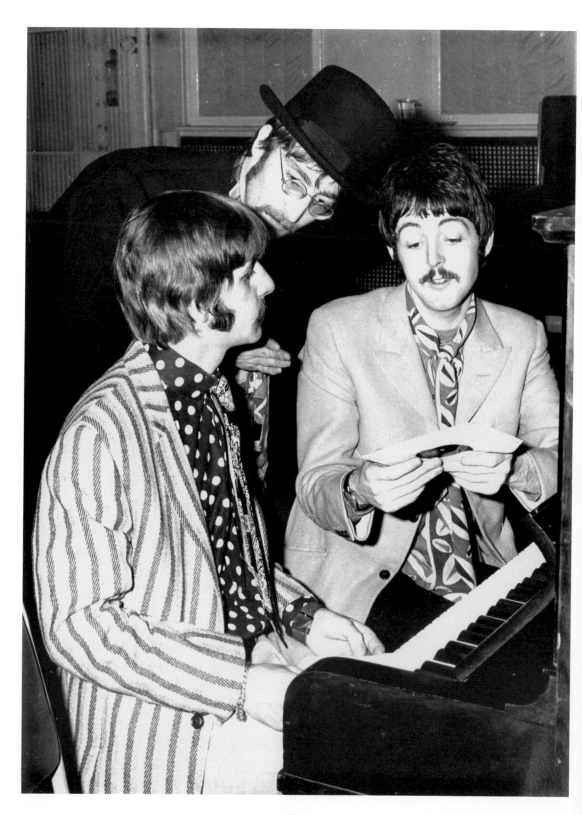

The Beatles' last ever Christmas Special for the BBC's Light Programme, and their last radio broadcast, went out at this time.

On Christmas Day itself George proposed to girlfriend Patti Boyd. She accepted and they became engaged.

Once again Christmas had arrived - another year of the legend had passed. As if to celebrate, "Paul McCartney's Christmas Album" (a specially pressed album of various bits of songs and readings) was produced. Only FOUR copies were pressed - these were given as presents to John, George, Ringo and Jane on 30th December.

On New Year's Eve a single "That's My Life" was issued by Freddie Lennon (John's father)- who had only recently returned to John's life. With respect to John it seemed 'with power like this' even knots in the wood could come out and they too would be famous!

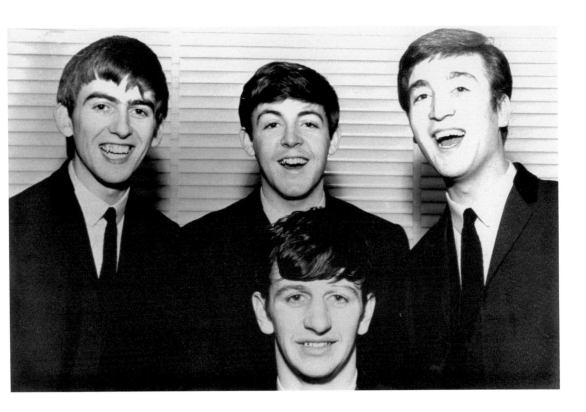

CHAPTER FIVE

"1966 - IT WAS JUST LIKE BEING IN A CIRCUS"

There was "NO". There still is a book available entitled "1966 And All That" which documents 1966 (in accordance with an American magazine of that time) as the major year of change within the Sixties era - and in fact that's just what it was.

For in 1966 a mood was being born which was going to change and influence not only music, but also fashion and graphics for many years to come - and The Beatles, who had been present all through it's conception and pregnancy, were to be there at the birth!

On January 21st George Harrison married model Patti Boyd in London, with Paul McCartney as the Best Man. Afterwards the couple flew off to honeymoon in Barbados whilst the press had a field day with Paul - after all Paul was the only bachelor left, the last 'free' Beatle. Who? When? Whatever the question, it sold newspapers.

Brian, on the other hand, started the year in his usual style by buying up Vic Lewis Management Ltd. thus giving him total control of eight of America's top acts, including Donovan, who was just getting his big break in the UK.

Meanwhile, back in Liverpool, things were not going too well for the city of its famous 'sons'. The Cavern Club, where Brian first discovered the group, was forced to close its doors on February 28th as a result of an unpaid £10,000 tax bill.

On March 4th the most controversial piece of press the group had experienced to date was to come from what was not really an interview. It was, in fact, a chat which John had with a journalist friend. Getting round to the subject of the Church's decline in the mid-Sixties, John was to state that in his opinion "The Beatles were bigger than Jesus..."

The next day saw instant headlines!

As for the music, at the start of April John and Paul made the decision to sell off their shares in Northern Songs Ltd. - they each received £146,000.

Back in America, Capitol (who you may remember weren't as quick to catch on

71

to the group as EMI in England) found themselves lagging behind yet again - two albums behind in fact. So, rather than issue three albums at once to make up for lost ground, they decided on a new 'beginning'. With special albums basically the best tracks from two became one and by June they were ready to issue a second album. However, Brian and the group were not too happy about this process - they felt it was 'butchering' their albums.

So, by way of protest, they were photographed for the sleeve wearing white doctor's coats with bits of meat and decapitated baby dolls strewn all over them. This was for the album "Yesterday and Today" (Rubber Soul/Revolver) which became known as the "Butcher Sleeve".

Because the cover was so macabre, Capitol were forced to withdraw the album after public outcry and change its sleeve, making it, of course, an instant 'collector's album', which has since been sold for anywhere between £850 and £1,200.

Returning to England George and Patti embarked on their first joint business venture - the opening of "Sybilla's", a disco in London.

Simultaneously, the Cavern Club in Liverpool had also located a saving source of cash via a new financial backer and re-opened its doors on July 23rd. Although The Beatles weren't present they did send a telegram wishing the new owners and staff "Good Luck with the continued success of the Club".

By now John's earlier comments on the Church were beginning to hit their mark politically. Brian had never liked politics and would always warn his acts that any crossover in the two fields of music and politics meant trouble with a capital 'T'. But as with The Beatles and many other artists the solution was not as 'black and white' as others would have them believe. An example was on July 29th, when the group pulled out of their planned tour of South Africa in support of their stand against Apartheid.

Like all things that happen when word breaks about a remark or comment from some famous person in England, it is only a matter of time before it reaches America (and vice versa). John's comment on Jesus was no different.

On July 31st his remark about the Church was published in the USA. Unlike England, where people were used to John, America went mad! This time there was immense public outcry. Radio stations banned Beatles records, and in the deep south the Klu Klux Klan organised huge fires for the burning of Beatles memorabilia.

Hearing the news about what was going on, Brian wanted desperately to cancel the Beatles' forthcoming tour of the USA. But the group were adamant about going ahead and Brian lost once again.

Arriving in America the group gave their first press conference on August 12th at which John apologised for his remarks. Later in the day Brian also granted the press a free hand and answered all their questions by adding his own personal apology, but not forgetting to tell the press that despite stories most concerts were sold out and ticket sales for the remainder were very good.

On August 19th the Klu Klux Klan did attempt to stop one of the concerts but failed. Most of the antagonisers were arrested.

Later in August (the 29th to be exact), Tony Barrow received a request from the group to film and record their evening show at Candlestick Park, San Francisco. (The show itself is still the private property of Paul McCartney and has never yet had a video release.) Although the group didn't yet know it, Candlestick Park was to be their last ever 'live' show. On the plane home George Harrison told one reporter "I am no longer a Beatle!"

Early September saw John leaving for Celle in West Germany to work on the movie "How I Won The War". It was a black comedy with Michael Crawford and was the first Beatle solo project. Years later John was to say "I knew it was over then, I just had to find a way out."

By this time all The Beatles were beginning to search for new directions in their lives.

On September 16th George and Patti left for a holiday in Rishnikesh, India. They were to join Indian musician Ravi Shankar and his family.

In October Paul started work on the film sound-track album for "The Family Way", a comedy movie starring Sir John Mills. This was to be the first Beatle solo album, although it is only conducted music written by Paul, with no words.

John, meanwhile, was about to start on a new chapter in his own life. On November 8th at London's Indica Gallery a show of destructive art opened. John was given a special preview of the show by gallery owner John Cadge. The artist ? Yoko Ono!

Whilst all the changes in their personal lives were beginning to happen, EMI had decided that The Beatles were ready for a new look professionally. Two days after the gallery show, EMI issued new press photos that shocked many of their loyal fans - the lovable 'mop-top' look had gone. All four Beatles now sported moustaches (in George's case a beard) and John, who had always admitted to being as blind as a bat, is seen wearing 'granny' glasses. It was for the first time in this guise that John was revealed to the public on Boxing Day in BBC2 TV's "Not Only But Also" with Peter Cook and Dudley Moore.

In December it was always EMI's policy to issue a new album from the group in order to hit the high sales Christmas market. But in 1966 there was no album ready. Consequently EMI decided to issue "A Collection of Beatles Oldies ... But Goldies". In a very modern psychedelic sleeve, it featured various hits from 1962-66 plus "Bad Boy" for the first time. This was supported on December 14th by the year's Fan Club Flexi, which was provided to all Fan Club members and entitled "Everywhere It's Christmas", with the sleeve having been designed by Paul.

As 1966 drew to a close the music business rumbled with rumours that the group were working on a theme album about their Liverpool childhood. However the rumours were initiated, the facts were that at Abbey Road The Beatles had 'open house' - being able to spend as much time (and money) as they wanted in order to make their next album! Time would prove that the wait and money spent was to be well worthwhile - as later years would testify!

CHAPTER SIX

"1967 - YOU STICK TO YOUR PERCENTAGES BRIAN, AND WE'LL HANDLE THE MUSIC"

In the mid-Seventies the team from BBC TV's "Blue Peter" buried a box outside BBC Television Centre in London. It was named "The Year 2000 Box" and contained various artefacts from the Sixties and Seventies so that when opened in 2000 A.D. it will show children of that year how the youth of the Sixties/Seventies era lived, what they read AND what they listened to.

Inside the box was a copy of the "Sgt. Pepper" album by The Beatles from 1967.

As a choice it was not surprising really as few albums can be found in the Top Ten 10 years (and even 20 YEARS) after their release - but "Sgt. Pepper" could! In fact few albums sell over 30 MILLION copies - but "Sgt. Pepper" did!

Only ONE album ever changed the way in which all other rock albums would be presented - with a 'gatefold' sleeve (never heard of before); lyrics printed on the sleeve (never heard of before); a printed inside sleeve (never heard of before) AND a free set of cardboard cut-outs (Guess what? Never heard of before!)

Only ONE album ever spent OVER ONE YEAR in the Number 1 position (never heard of before - or since).

The Album ...? "SGT. PEPPER'S LONELY HEARTS CLUB BAND" !

The Group ...? THE BEATLES ! (as if you hadn't guessed!)

The early part of 1967 saw several business changes starting with, in January, NEMS Enterprises merging with the Robert Stigwood Group and making Brian the manager of FOUR other groups, including The Who.

On January 30th a concert was given at Brian's Saville Theatre by Jimi Hendrix. Brian was at the show with John and Paul at his side and Hendrix was fast to become the No. 1 guitar hero in the world.

As the year rolled into February, the group's contract with EMI/Capitol came up

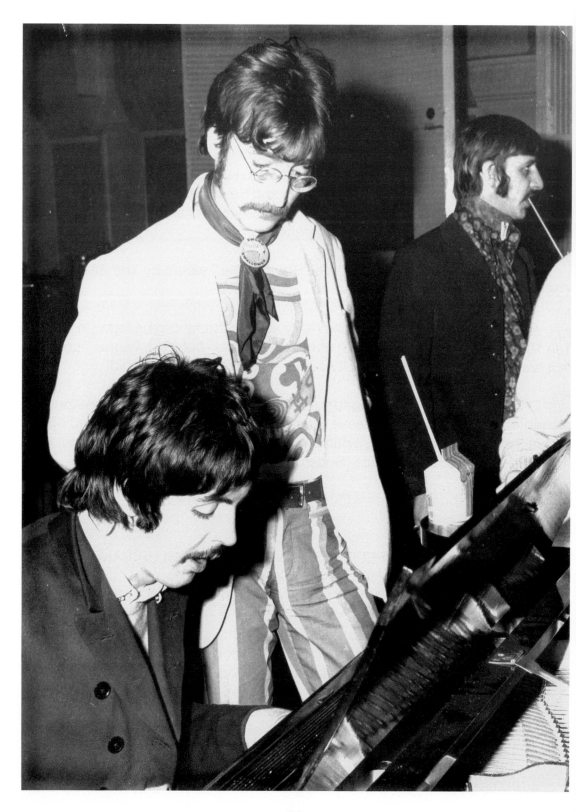

for renewal. But the companies had little to fear after having given the group such a free hand in the previous few months. The Beatles re-signed a further NINE YEAR recording contract deal which was to take them to 1976.

Capitol, by this time, had been pushing EMI for a new single. The American market hadn't had one for some considerable time - there just wasn't anything around, not until George Martin was told! As the first two tracks were finished they were packaged and released with (for the first time again!) a Beatles-conceived promotional video for each - "Strawberry Fields" and "Penny Lane".

On February 9th 1967 'Psychadelia' was truly born when the BBC showed both videos for the first time.

After a relatively quiet remainder of the month (except for Brian paying £35,000 for Rushlake Green, a manor house once owned by Sir Winston Churchill), the group focused their energies towards their next album.

On March 30th, within a London photographic studio owned by top photographer Michael Cooper, the group posed for their next sleeve with cut-outs and wax models in military uniforms. They kept the lid on so tightly that the photo session was classed 'Top Secret' and done behind locked doors.

The week after, on April 5th, Paul flew out to Denver, Colorado, with Beatles' 'roadie' Mal Evans to be with Jane Asher on her 21st birthday. On the return flight a few days later Paul wrote the words "Magical Mystery Tour" on a brown paper bag, telling Mal that it would come in handy for a very special project.

Although Paul didn't indicate anything more it was obvious that he had other projects in mind. Because of this compulsion for other projects by all the members of the group, April 19th saw the formation of a new corporation known as "The Beatles and Co." to cover the legal aspects of all future projects.

With no more tours, Brian had been having more and more trouble in keeping himself busy, his job giving him less and less to do and he was becoming increasingly dependent on sleeping pills. He didn't seem to have any positive say in the group's activities anymore. In fact, at on studio session he broke in on the intercom and said something to Paul about re-doing the bass line. John, in his typical fashion, shouted back "You stick to your f!!!!!!! percentages Brian, we'll handle the music ... right!"

John had been approached by Brian to get the band back on the road but once again, in typical Lennon fashion, his answer was given not to Brian but to the press "no more tours, no more mop tops, just Beatles."

The Beatles were moving into a new era, further heralded by John in May when a white Rolls Royce he had bought in 1964 was then painted to look like a psychedelic gypsy caravan by a group of hippy Greek designers known as 'The Fool'.

This was followed on June 1st by the release of the album "Sgt. Pepper's Lonely Hearts Club Band". For Brian it had been a nightmare - its cover (a collage of famous faces stood with the group) took an age to assemble. EMI's lawyers had withdrawn Jesus Christ, Adolf Hitler and Mahatma Ghandi for all the right reasons. Of course the group wanted other things never even thought of before - like the lyrics to all songs being printed on the sleeve. This also gave the EMI lawyers ulcers, but they managed it.

In America Capitol issued it as an album which was another first, although they were to follow suit with all other albums from that point on.

It was of course a masterpiece, all the hours of hard work had paid off. The group had now sold themselves to an audience in such a way that even people who had until then written off The Beatles as a craze were buying the album. It became the 'Best Selling Album of All Time' and wasn't given any other challenge for over sixteen years - and only then from Michael Jackson's "Thriller".

Their change in direction also took The Beatles into rather close proximity with other 'fads' of the sixties era - namely drugs.

On June 19th Paul made a statement to the press that he had used the drug 'LSD' on a number of occasions. The album also contained a song called "Lucy In The Sky With Diamonds", which the press had decided stood for 'LSD'. The truth of the matter was that young Julian had taken home a drawing from school of a lady who was flying amongst the stars. When John asked what it was the young lad replied "Lucy in the sky with diamonds", and on that John wrote the song.

NB: Although the song's initials are obviously "LITSWD" rather than "LSD", when the press want stories it seems that some of them don't always notice those 'little' inaccuracies.

In the USA and then the UK, the use of the soft drug Marijuana was becoming more and more commonplace amongst the youth of the country. So much so that quite a few people (including some notable MPs) were calling for legislation of the drug. On July 24th The Times carried a full page advertisement calling for the legal use of the drug. Among the stars who put their names to the advertisement were The Beatles together with Brian.

Some groups would never have known how to follow an album like "Sgt. Pepper" but The Beatles had kept an 'ace up their sleeve' even before the "Sgt. Pepper" album was released.

"Our World" was to be a worldwide TV link-up. For the first time ever 400 million viewers would all see the same show. Who had been asked to appear on behalf of the UK - who else but The Beatles!

For the occasion the group came up with "All You Need Is Love" as an anthem for world peace and unity. The song was recorded 'live' from Abbey Road on the TV show with a sing-a-long chorus of rock stars and friends.

The new era for the group was constantly changing. Mysticism and foreign cultures were fast becoming a focal point of attention. On her last trip to India with George, Patti had made acquaintance with the Maharishi Myesh Yogi, an Indian Guru who introduced her to meditation. On August 24th the Maharishi arrived in England and Patti introduced him to John, Paul and George.

On August 25th the group and their wives (or Jane in Paul's case) left for a trip to Bangor in North Wales to attend the Guru's classes on meditation at his camp. Cynthia was late and missed the train but was driven down the next day by Neil Aspinall. Amongst the others to go to Wales were The Rolling Stones, Donovan and The Beach Boys; the craze (or was it education) was spreading.

Their peace, however, was utterly shattered two days later.

Brian was supposed to be following them to Wales later that week. By then his pill-taking had got worse. He had left his London office to go to his stately home where he had gone straight to bed with the bedroom door locked. Later in the day his housekeeper discovered that she couldn't get any answer from his room. After calls were made to and from the office, Alistair Taylor arrived with Peter Brown. A doctor was called and the door was broken down - but it was too late. At 32, after an accidental overdose of pills and drink, Brian Epstein was dead.

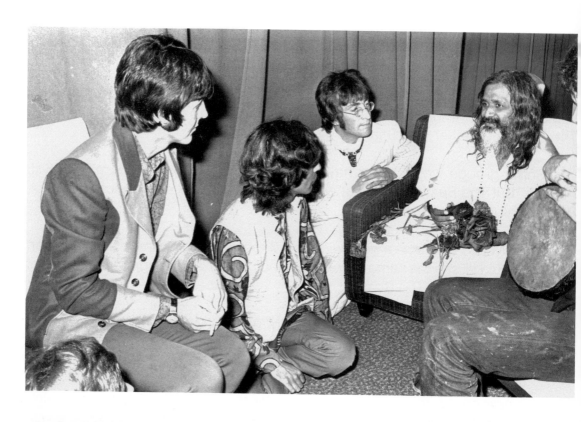

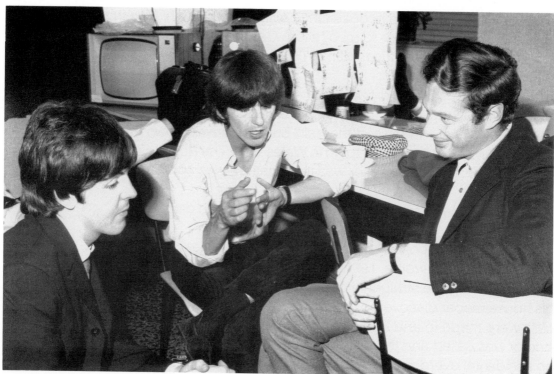

The group returned to London at once. In order to avoid undue and upsetting publicity for the family The Beatles did not attend the funeral of Brian at Kirkdale Jewish Cemetery, Long Lane, Liverpool. The group did, however, attend a full Memorial Service at London's Jewish Synagogue. Brian's management contract with the group was signed for five years in 1962; alive or dead, the grim reality was that it was set up for renewal. Many people have since said that had Brian lived the group may not have stayed with him anyway. Without the touring what could he have done for them?

As if to confirm this, on September 1st Clive Epstein (Brian's brother) took over the management of NEMS Enterprises Ltd. and on the same day The Beatles announced that they would no longer require the services of NEMS as they were going to go ahead and manage themselves. Brian's death was a bitter blow for everyone but the show had to go on - it had to be business as usual (well almost). On October 7th Sid Bernstein, the New York based promoter, offered the group $1 million to make 2 comeback shows at Shea Stadium. He was turned down.

Paul's "Magical Mystery Tour" plan was the group's way of getting over Brian's death; a one hour TV Movie for which the group filled a coach with families, friends, animals and circus freaks and travelled round filming whatever happened - unfortunately nothing did! Its sound-track EP (Double) which went with a free book was good music which almost echoed "Sgt. Pepper" and sold well. The movie, however, was not as fortunate. It was given a TV premiere on BBC2 on Boxing Day. It had cost the BBC £20,000 for the copyright of Applefilms' first production, and it was shown in black and white - the press had a field day!

For the first time The Beatles could be criticised and boy did they turn the knife! It was proved in no uncertain terms that the group were no longer the 'darlings' of the press. The next couple of months were fairly quiet and it wasn't until early December that Ringo left for Rome to work on the movie "Candy" in which he played Emmanuel the Gardener. This was followed by John and Paul announcing to the press that their new self-management company was to be called Apple Corps Ltd., a business who's intent was to produce Records, Movies, Art and Fashion as well as taking time to discover and record new up-and-coming bands. Apple opened its doors at 94 Baker Street, London with the Apple Boutique.

By then another year had gone by. It was 'Flexi Disc' time again and on December 11th the 1967 flexi "Christmastime Is Here Again" was issued to all Fan Club members - this time with the sleeve designed by 4 1/2 year old Julian whilst the New York photographer Linda Eastman took photo shots of John, Paul and George in London. As if to round off the year on a happy note, and after having been together through everything, Paul and Jane finally got engaged on Christmas Day with rumours of a summer wedding.

But 1967 had not been a kind year ...

From there on in The Beatles were to have something to prove if they were to remain at the top - and they were on their own!

CHAPTER SEVEN

1968 - "IT'S LIKE PUTTING FOUR SOLO ALBUMS ON ONE RECORD"

How in the world does any group follow a year in which their album sold more copies than there are people in Australia, and yet also a year when the press finally found a way to criticise them. With Brian gone and their future firmly in their own hands, it was now up to The Beatles and they were now most definitely on their own on this one.

The group's year started on January 5th with the re-showing by the BBC (this time in colour) of the "Magical Mystery Tour". What on earth the 'Beeb' hoped to achieve by this God only knows. The press thought Christmas had come again twelve months early as they gave the movie and the band another slagging. What is strange is that in these days (i.e. 1988) "Mystery Tour" was one of the USA's best selling videos. It is the only place where film of the band can be found playing "I Am The Walrus" and at the time of writing this book most art magazines still review it as 'years ahead of its time'.

Even stranger still was the fact that on February 5th Paul booked the Royal Garden Hotel in London for a press conference - and then failed to turn up.

During this period Japanese artist Yoko Ono had been seeing more and more of John. The fact that he was married did not appear to have been a problem because so was she - the only law (and it was the Great Unwritten Law) was that NO wives or girlfriends ever entered the recording studio - this was the 'inner sanctum', 'all for one and one for all' ... the four musketeers!

However, on February 11th John broke the rule and took Yoko along to the recording session for "Hey Bulldog". Needless to say, the others were not amused.

From a publicity point of view the group's image was sagging. Mid-February saw London journalist Hunter Davis commissioned by the group to write their official biography - a task he accepted there and then.

In addition to this, on March 29th Derek Taylor (the man Brian once appointed as his Press Officer), was appointed to the same position at Apple and the company's first offices opened on April 3rd at 95 Wigmore Street, London. Later the same month Derek placed a large advertisement in the New Musical Express inviting unknown musicians to send tapes to Apple and become famous - the office was snowed under with replies. Business as usual - at last!

In early May Cynthia and Julian went on holiday to Greece with Donovan. They arrived home at Weybridge to find Yoko Ono naked except for a small bath robe. Cyn was understandably extremely upset and went off to stay with her mother. On May 16th John asked Cynthia for a divorce.

As for Yoko, she was now to be seen at every group recording session and always right at John's side. On May 30th she actually recorded with the group a number entitled "Revolution Number 9" - a 9 minute recording of gibberish which was far nearer to Yoko's idea of conceptual art than anything which the group had ever done. George wanted the track nowhere near the next album!

From a record sales standpoint The Beatles were still very much in demand but now they had their own company new agreements had to be reached. On June 20th the first of these agreements was solidified when EMI/Parlophone finally agreed that all future records by The Beatles could be released on Apple (through EMI, of course). It was further agreed that the Agreement would continue until 1976 when they would switch the Catalogue back to EMI - a clause in the contract that EMI didn't mind agreeing to as at that point no one foresaw the group still being together anyway.

To assist with the extra load on the studios at Apple the group paid £500,000 on June 22nd for 3 Saville Row, London. They then planned to turn the basement into a recording studio and the rest into the company's new offices.

A week later further publicity was afforded the group when John opened up his first Art Exhibition "You Are Here" on July 1st. Although all the group were invited only John and Yoko attended.

Only one last remnant of Brian's management remained - that was the commission to make an animated film about The Beatles. The subject was of total horror to the group as the only track record they had experienced of anything similar was "The Flintstones". But United Artists were still pushing for a third movie (their original contract being for three, and only two having been made so far). So, thinking it would fulfil their contract, the group said yes.

The Beatles actually supplied very little to the film. The voices were done by actors and 85% of the music was old numbers - it was an animated fantasy called "Yellow Submarine". But on seeing the 'rough cut' they actually liked it and subsequently supplied a personal ending to it. The movie was actually premiered on July 17th in London with Ringo and George Harrison attending with their wives, John taking Yoko and Paul going alone ... (obviously the summer wedding was off!)

In response the critics liked it and it won back some of the goodwill that "Mystery Tour" had lost for them.

Once again it was time for a change in business direction. At the end of July the Apple Boutique closed its doors and gave away £20,000 worth of stock to passers-by and charities. On August 7th Paul ordered that the windows be blacked out and the words "Hey Jude" (a new concept in single records) be written upon them in white paint.

On August 11th Apple announced 'National Apple Week' to help promote the company but no one took much notice except for one daily paper who called it 'National Non Event Week.' For others that may have been extremely disconcerting, but The Beatles were different.

In early September they issued "Hey Jude", a single, and the first record on their Apple label. It was unusual in that it had a running time of over 7 minutes, totally uncommon to radio play in which most records were only of a 3 minute duration. But once again The Beatles were the exception to the rule and "Hey Jude" became the group's biggest ever selling single. For its video the group invited 60 Fan Club members to Twickenham Studios where they performed a kind of sing-a-long version in the same style as "All You Need Is Love" for the "Our World" TV show.

Following John's breaking of the unwritten law, Paul (then dating New York photographer Linda Eastman) took Linda to a recording session on September 18th. Whether this inspired him or not we don't know. But what we DO know is that on October 11th a new single was issued by the Bonzo Dog Doo-Da Band and called "I'm the Urban Spaceman". It was produced by someone called Apollo C. Vermouth (you've guessed it - none other than Paul McCartney!)

But the group's image was dealt a severe blow once again when seven days later, in the early hours of the morning at their flat, John and Yoko were the subject of a degrading police raid. Whether justified or not, the police found 219 grams of cannabis resin. John always claimed it was only a plant but the couple were found guilty and fined £150 with £20 costs.

Not to be outdone, Apple issue "Two Virgins", an album from John and Yoko with the sleeve containing a full frontal nude photo of the two of them, whilst the actual content of the album was just various weird electronic noises. For purposes of trying not to get the album an immediate ban, all copies were issued in brown paper bags with peep-holes for the couple's faces. When the press rang Apple for comment the only Beatle available was Ringo, who's only comment was "... don't worry, it's just John being John!"

November 22nd was the day when the world received the follow up to "Sgt. Pepper" and called simply "The Beatles". The two album set had an ironic title inasmuch as it was the group's least-like effort to date. Having recorded some songs on a solo basis and others with friends, including Eric Clapton. During the album's completion there appeared to be so much contradiction that Ringo walked out and left the group - only to be coaxed back later.

The album itself came in a plain white sleeve with fans soon nicknaming it "The White Album". It was issued with a free 8" x 10" colour shot of each group member and a poster featuring a collage on one side and a complete set of lyrics on the other, In addition George Martin lost his battle as the Yoko-influenced track of "Revolution Number 9" did appear on the album. The album sold quite quickly, but word out on the street (both in and out of the music business) was that The Beatles had lost it!

On November 28th, only six days after one album, came another; because of legal problems and packaging requirements the "Yellow Submarine" film sound-track album was finally issued. Then, as with previous years, time seemed to catch up on them. It was December yet again ...

As if events of the past year hadn't made their mark, on December 18th, John and Yoko decided to once again protest in support of world peace by lying on the stage in a black bag at The Royal Albert Hall. Although a worthy cause, it was once again an opportunity for the world's press to 'get their knives in'. Similarly also to previous years, December 20th highlighted "The '68 Christmas Record" which was as usual issued free to all Fan Club Members. The difference this year was that all group members had recorded their segments separately, and of course Yoko Ono participated. Yoko's increasing participation in affairs was further pronounced when on December 23rd she and John both dressed up as Santa Claus and distributed presents to staff at the Apple Christmas Party.So 1968 came to what must have been considered by some to be a welcome end. The question on everybody's lips was 'would the group make it through another year.' In reality it was felt that the rot was beginning to set in - and nobody knew the cure!

CHAPTER EIGHT

"1969 - THIS JUST HAS TO BE IT, WE'VE ALL GOT FAMILIES"

When you've spent the last seven years climbing to the top of the tree, when you've picked apples from every branch on the way, what on earth do you do to follow it?

In 1969 Man first set foot on the Moon. The only outstanding fact was that it wasn't The Beatles, after all they'd conquered every other possible feat.

But, for the group that had done everything, the biggest feat that they could pull off in '69 would be to get through the year.

At the start of the year in the USA 30,000 copies of "Two Virgins" were confiscated by police under the American Pornography Laws. It was of course expected to happen somewhere sometime, but was not the best start to the year.

This inauspicious beginning was further aggravated on January 10th when, after a rather heated argument with Paul, George walked out of the session saying that he was leaving the group.

At that time they were only part way through filming "Let It Be", the third movie they still owed to United Artists. After being mistaken in thinking that "Yellow Submarine" would have fulfilled the 3 film contract they discovered that as a cartoon it didn't count.

During the same period John was also unsettled and on January 18th made a statement to the press saying "Apple is in a financial mess. If it carries on like this we could be bankrupt in two years."

Thankfully things were patched up and John coaxed George back to the studio. With Paul deciding that a good part for the film would be to go 'live' on the Apple roof at Saville Row, January 30th saw the group climbing on to the roof about midday and performing about five numbers 'live'- after all wasn't the good thing about The Beatles the fact that they could always 'cut it live'?

- at least until the Police shut them down because of the noise!

"Let It Be" did take its toll however, and after 30 days filming, in which 28 hours of film covering 70 songs had been finished, the project known as "Let It Be" was shelved. No-one in the group or their entourage (including George Martin) could face any more.

Allen Klein was a short, fat, shabby-looking guy who had recently helped out The Rolling Stones. On February 3rd, figuring that he was the only one who could possibly save the 'rotting Apple', the Beatles appointed Allen as their manager.

The next day the New York law firm Eastman and Eastman (Linda's father and brother) were asked to legally represent the group.

At last things seemed to be taking a positive 'upturn' - but only until February 22nd when the "Sgt. Pepper" album finally slipped to No. 3 in the Charts after a record breaking 88 weeks at No. 1.

Unfortunately it came at a time when everything else also seemed to be slipping - and fast!

On February 28th came the day when the group had to put their names to Allen Klein's contract. John, George and Ringo all signed straight away. Paul, on the other hand, didn't want to sign with Klein and so signed a management contract with Lee Eastman instead.

The connection to the Eastman family was strongly bonded and family links were more formally cemented when on March 12th Paul and Linda were married at a London Register Office after a very brief 3 to 4 week engagement. Mal Evans and Peter Brown were witnesses with Heather (Linda's daughter by her first marriage) as Bridesmaid. Of note was Mike McCartney who, as Best Man was late but did eventually turn up.

On the same day, as if to prove that one Beatle's happiness is not another's, George and his wife Patti were arrested on drugs charges and later fined £250.

These hiccups did not prevent business continuing and Allen Klein, having started his new appointment at the beginning of March, was busily trying to separate the group from NEMS Enterprises, who by that time weren't offering The Beatles any services of any kind and yet fully owned millions of pounds in Royalties.

Five days after Paul's wedding Sir Lew Grade bought his old friend Dick James'

37% of Northern Songs to put into his new TV company ATV. This now meant that the original four partners had no hand whatsoever in the future of Northern Songs Ltd.

So much for changing fortunes!

As if Paul's wedding had started a new craze, Peter Brown then followed up his term of office as Best Man with a second wedding on 21st March; he was Best Man at John and Yoko's wedding in Gibraltar.

Being well know exhibitionists, John and Yoko decided to use their honeymoon, and any other press and publicity they might get, by lying in a hotel bedroom in Amsterdam - in support of world peace.

This was followed by a further press release on APRIL 1ST when John told the press that he and Yoko were to have sex change operations - at least 2 newspapers didn't notice the date and ran the stories. Press 0 Beatles 1!

The press did however get a story on April 22nd when, on the roof of the Apple Building, John Winston Lennon changed his name by Deed Poll to John Ono Lennon. Witness at the quick ceremony was Yoko Ono Lennon.

By now a third of the year had gone by and things had been hectic. May was no different.

The first of May saw Apple announce a new label "Zapple Records". It was to be totally exclusive and used for records which EMI gave them trouble with, like "Two Virgins". The label was firstly to handle "Electronic Sounds" (a solo album of just that by George) and "Life With The Lions" (the weird and equally strange follow-up to "Two Virgins".)

On May 5th John and Yoko paid £150,000 for their new home Tittenhurst Park, where they were to stay until their move to America. (Ringo was to later buy the house in 1973.)

But two days later it was back to business.

John and Paul had for once been in agreement when, on May 7th, they used Allen Klein as middle man to ask EMI for a larger share of royalties for Apple - EMI agreed.

Albert Dock, Liverpool.

Abbey Road, London.

The day after John, George and Ringo once again tried to get Paul to sign with Allen Klein by putting their 75% of Apple into Klein's hands. But again Paul turned them down and, as if in some kind of protest, Alistair Taylor (Brian's personal assistant since 1961 and good close friend of Paul) was fired on the spot. Paul still refused to budge.

On May 26th John and Yoko formed their own publishing company called "Bag Productions Ltd."

Meanwhile John and Paul were still writing and the next Beatles single featured only John and Paul on the A-side with the full group on the B-side. The single was known as "The Ballad of John and Yoko", with Paul playing drums and bass while John handled guitar and vocals.

The Plastic Ono Band, who were fast becoming John's new band, followed this with an issue of their own first single "Give Peace A Chance".

Because of not being able to change any 'legalistics' Klein had to accept that the label credit still had to be Lennon-McCartney.

Abbey Road Studios, St. John's Wood, London (or Studio Number 2 at the aforementioned place to be more exact) was where The Beatles had recorded almost everything in their history. So when Paul managed to coax the others back to make yet another album (in effect to be their last) everybody, including George Martin, thought the best title for it would be "Abbey Road".

So between 9 a.m. and 11 a.m. on August 8th, the road was closed whilst the group were photographed walking across the zebra crossing - thus making it one of London's most famous landmarks. (Author's note: In 1989 a traffic warden was reported to say that no other crossing in London was used more.)

By the end of August, the other members of the group were getting irritated at Paul's constant refusals and decided that they were going to try and get him out of the group. At a private meeting in the Apple offices on August 31st John, George and Ringo tried to come up with a possible replacement. They all agreed on Bob Dylan. Mal Evans, one of the group's road crew was given the job of asking. But Bob Dylan had also seen the stories like everyone else in the world and knew the group wasn't going to last long. Not surprisingly he turned the chance down.

John carried on to play the Toronto Peace Festival in Canada on September 13th. It was his stage comeback and on that occasion his ever-changing Plastic Ono Band consisted of Eric Clapton, Klaus Voorman, Alan White, John and of course Yoko.

Next on September 20th Northern Songs ownership was published with ATV owning 50%, Paul 30%, John 15% and Ringo 5%. George had no shares whatsoever in the company.

By this time rumours had become rife!

So much so that in the first weeks of October and in America (it could only happen in America!) a D.J. came up with the story that Paul was DEAD! - he even gave good reasons to support his claim.

In the following paragraphs we highlight some of the points that led to his claim and let you the readers decide for yourselves:

a) Apparently Paul had died in 1967 and had been replaced with Billy Shears (a Paul look-a-like).b) If people listened to the record "Strawberry Fields" John could be heard saying "I buried Paul".
c) The "Sgt. Pepper" Album sleeve had its own fair share of clues - namely:
1) Raised hand of Paul behind head was Indian death sign.
2) Paul's arm band "OPD" stood for "Officially Pronounced Dead".
3) On the back of the album Paul had his back to the camera because it wasn't him, someone else stood in for him.
d) On the "Magical Mystery Tour" album:
1) Paul wore a black rose on the sleeve while all the others wore red ones, a clear sign that Billy Shears was mourning his predecessor's passing.
e) On the "White Album":
1) Play certain songs backwards and they have hidden messages about Paul's death.
f) On the "Abbey Road Album":
1) Car number plate 28 IF. If Paul had lived in 1969 he would have been 28.
2) Funeral procession on the cover shows John (the Vicar) in white; Ringo (the Mourner) in black; George (the Gravedigger) in denims and Paul in a two piece black suit with no shoes and socks (the Italian way of being buried).

For the first time ever, and in this book, we thought we would like to shed some light on the subject with some of our personal explanations to some of the above well publicised but totally implausible claims. So we'll start at the beginning and you, the reader, can follow on by making up your own minds.

a) The message at the end of "Strawberry Fields" is in fact "Cranberry Sauce"not "I buried Paul".

b) On the "Sgt. Pepper album:

1) The raised hand could have been behind anybody as over 20 photos were taken on the set with the group sitting or standing in various poses around the cut outs and wax figures, the actual photo used could have been any one.

2) "OPD" actually stood for "Official Police Department" and the arm band came from 'Granny Takes a Trip', a psychedelic clothes shop.

3) Same as No. 1 where many photos were available to choose from.

c) On "Magical Mystery Tour" album:

1) The black rose was a joke.

d) On the "White Album":

1) Just play the tracks backwards yourselves and you'll see the gobbledegook that plays the right way is even more weird (as well as incomprehensible) when played backwards.

e) On the "Abbey Road" album:

1) Same as "Sgt. Pepper" album - option of many photos.

2) Well the group wore whatever they wanted. Paul lived round the corner at Cavendish Road and it was a hot summer's day. In some of the shots (see 'Return to Abbey Road' bootleg) he is wearing sandals.

3) In Italy they bury people in white shrouds as elsewhere.

And on and on we go ...!

On November 7th Paul told the press that reports of his death had been greatly exaggerated and that when it DID happen he'd make sure they knew about it.

Meanwhile any news is good news for sales ...!

The following day Capitol (in USA) reported to the press that since the reports of Paul's death, Beatle album sales had improved by 40%, just going to prove that you CAN fool some of the people some of the time.

Anyway, enough of this drivel and back to our book ...

Ever the eccentric, John and Yoko bought an island off the coast of Ireland called Dornish; they then gave it to a group of homeless hippies.

John and Yoko were both known to stand up for admirable causes throughout the world (albeit in a somewhat unusual manner) and it was just as evident on November 25th when John returned his MBE to the Queen. He stated that he was returning it because of Britain's blindness toward the Vietnam War and because "Cold Turkey" had slipped in the charts. (" Cold Turkey" was the new Plastic Ono Band single.)

John and Yoko's continual messages arose again on December 10th when they both demanded a retrial for convicted killer James Hanratty. Having spoken to his parents they believed him to be innocent. However, they failed and he was executed.

Christmas was looming ahead ...

December 11th was the day that American concert promoter Mike Belkin offered the group $2.4 million to play a one-off Christmas gig in the States. It was no surprise to anyone that he was turned down.

Then, on December 15th, came a decision by ITV to film a TV special called "Man of the Decade"; John Lennon was to be that man!

By now Christmas, which had become a very personal family time in the lives of the group, was only a week away. Once again they wanted to do something for the fans and once again it was the Christmas 'flexi' - the seventh.

Because of the pressure than on the group they didn't really want to continue recording together for records, and so the seventh 'flexi' was to be their last. In 1972, though, all Fan Club Members received "From Then to US" a proper hard vinyl album featuring the contents of all the flexis from 1962-69.

With 1969 drawing to a close the subject of The Beatles as a group was one which many people were beginning to question. Will they record again ? When will news of their split be announced? Could anyone save them ?

The next year was to be the start of a new decade.

The group had dominated the Sixties, but could they survive the Seventies ?

CHAPTER NINE

"1970 - I'M SORRY LADS IT'S OVER"

What could anybody do? How do you stop the inevitable happening? Should you even try?

When The Beatles formed they were four young lads. Now they were married with wives and children to consider. Hadn't John always said "I won't be singing 'She Loves You' when I'm 30", and how old was he in 1970 - 30!

The question nobody could answer was what impact were the most famous four Sons of the Sixties going to have on the Seventies? Moreover, could they even get through the first year of the new decade?

On January 14th George and Patti paid well over £100,000 for Friar Park, a 30 room Gothic mansion in Henley-on-Thames.

Two days later John was once again the subject of a police raid - this time on one of his art exhibitions entitled "Bag One", which was said to be pornographic. By then John was also working much more closely with Yoko than he was with The Beatles - so much so that he next made an announcement to the press that from then on 1970 was going to be known as Year One!

The following day Ringo and Maureen were expected to fly to Los Angeles with Peter Brown for the American premiere of Ringo's new movie "Magic Christian". Peter booked an airport press conference for Ringo. But instead of being asked solely about the film, Ringo was bombarded with questions about The Beatles which he refused to answer; he would only comment on "Magic Christian".

Records and albums once again became topical with the issue of a new single on February 6th by The Plastic Ono Band called "Instant Karma" and backed on the B-side by a guitar solo on a number called "Who Has Seen The Wind" by George Harrison. After all, it was not uncommon by this point for members of the group to help out friends, even best friends to their 'Circle of Four.'

As for the 'majors', Capitol were on the warpath once more. When was the new album out? Where's the next single? and by late February they were screaming for a Beatles Album.

But there just wasn't an album to give - and the mass of tapes known as "Let It Be" had still not been edited. So "Hey Jude" was issued - a collection of singles not previously issued on any album. Oh yes it was another famous 'butcher job' but by then neither EMI nor the group could give a damn.

This was followed on March 6th by the first single from "Let It Be" (in fact the title track). The group themselves weren't too bothered as they had had little to do with its mixing or packaging. No one then knew that it was to be The Beatles' last single!

During this period it was no secret that Paul had been working on his own solo album at his home studio. He wanted to put together an interview of himself to be included in all promo and D.J. copies of the Album. In the interview he claimed that he and The Beatles had parted company. Somehow the Daily Mirror got hold of a copy and on April 10th it was front page news.

Two days later Paul announced the forming of his own company McCartney Productions Ltd. (to be known as MPL). The company's first job was to purchase the rights to the Daily Express cartoon strip "Rupert Bear" which Paul intended to make into a cartoon film - they completed the purchase on April 14th.

The rest of April was somewhat unsensational except for a judge ruling, on April 27th, that John's "Bag One" was not pornographic. Consequently his lithographs which had been seized in the earlier raid were returned to him.

After months running through the "Let It Be" tapes, Phil Spector finally cleaned them up, sorted out what was useful and what wasn't, and added his own distinct 'wall of sound'. So, on May 8th, EMI finally issued the "Let It Be" album. Proof that the project was originally shelved before it was finished can be plainly heard on the album as the group crack jokes before some songs and are heard to 'count themselves in' on others. The end to the Sixties' most popular group has tended to be marked with "Abbey Road", which was recorded after, but issued before "Let It Be" - the group's final swansong.

"Let It Be" the movie was finally premiered in London on May 13th. The group didn't turn up but anyone who did could see why. The movie showed a band splitting up, walkouts, arguments on screen; it was 90 minutes of dirty laundry on film for all to see!

Had Brian been alive to see the film he would have cried - his boys had finally started to hurt each other (something he had never wanted). The split up of The Beatles was beginning to gather momentum. But by then the story was becoming an accepted fact rather than a question - it didn't even sell papers anymore (as the Daily Express proved when, on May 20th, it issued a cover story stating that The Beatles as a group no longer existed).

Another sign of the split came on June 11th when John and Yoko told the press that they were going to be making New York their home from that point on. Repercussions were starting to take effect. Four days later (back in the UK) Paul's father-in-law, Lee Eastman, sent a letter to Allen Klein suggesting that although the group were contractually obliged to remain as a unit until 1976, they should be officially dissolved immediately.

On August 4th Apple's press section was closed down and all its staff were fired. Well without a press section what else could they do? All they could do as just a label was issue records and EMI were doing that for them already. It seemed that the Apple had not been such a good idea after all (as Adam said to Eve!)

Allen Klein did not reply to Lee Eastman's letter and so Paul wrote to John asking him to break up The Beatles. John replied saying that he would only consider it when George and Ringo had their say. By the end of August Paul was still nowhere with his plea and so, in the face of all the publicity, he sent the following letter to Melody Maker:

"*Dear Sir,*
In order to put out of its misery the limping dog of a news story which has been dragging itself across your page for the past year, my answer to the question 'will The Beatles get together again?' is 'NO'!

Signed Paul McCartney."

On August 29th the magazine used the letter as its cover story.

In September John and Paul added further fuel to the fire when they filed a lawsuit against Northern Songs demanding half the firm's income and capital dating back to 1963. The final nail in the coffin came on November 15th, when Paul filed al lawsuit against John, George, Ringo, Klein and Appleto officially dissolve the group. The case took 5 years to decide but on January 5th 1975 a judge ruled:
....THE ENTITY ONCE KNOWN AS THE BEATLES NO LONGER EXISTED....

CHAPTER TEN

"IT COULD NEVER HAPPEN AGAIN ... AND NEVER WITH JULIAN"

And so it was over, the most respected band of the Sixties had split. The Seventies and onwards were only to feel their influence. But what about a reunion? Couldn't they pull it off just once more?

By January 19th 1971 The Beatles & Co. Partnership (one of their companies) had been dissolved by the High Court.

REUNION NUMBER 1 - On August 1st 1971 George Harrison invited various top musicians to play Madison Square Gardens in New York. The Concert for Bangladesh (the ultimate forerunner to Live Aid) was a way of raising money for the poor and starving people of Bangladesh. John was invited but turned it down when he realised that Yoko wasn't. Contrary to popular rumour Paul wasn't even asked. In the end only Ringo joined his old mate live on stage.

March 31st 1972 - The Official Beatles UK Fan Club was closed down after having lost 70% of its members over the previous 4 years.

REUNION NUMBER 2 - The only real reunion - and even then all four group members weren't in the studio at the same time. But everyone one could be heard playing on various tracks on the "Ringo" album and in fact there are songs on that same album written by Lennon, Harrison and/or McCartney.

November 28th 1974 - Terribly nervous, but keeping to his promise, John made a guest appearance at Madison Square Gardens with Elton John. It was obviously not known at the time that this was John's last ever live stage appearance.

January 26th 1976 - The group's 9-year recording contract with EMI ended. Paul stayed with the label but George signed to A & M who were to distribute his Dark Horse Label. Ringo signed to Polydor, and John, then retired, didn't sign with anyone.

April 1976 - John announced that he was going to retire from the music scene to be with his newborn son Sean Taro Ono Lennon.

REUNION NUMBER 3 - On September 20th 1976 Sid Bernstein, the

US promoter offered the group $230 MILLION for a one-off reunion concert. He was turned down.

April 27th 1979 - Allen Klein was found guilty of tax evasion and sent to jail. The said taxes related to his time with The Beatles.

REUNION NUMBER 4 - Sid Bernstein was at it again when, on September 9th 1979, he offered a staggering $500 MILLION for a one night stand in New York. You'd think that by then he would know the answer!

November 17th 1980 - John Lennon and Yoko Ono issued their comeback album "Double Fantasy" through Griffin.

December 8th 1980 - 11.07 p.m. - John arrived back at the Dakota Building (his home in New York). At the building entrance a 'fan', Mark David Chapman, pumped five bullets into him at close range. He was rushed to hospital but pronounced dead on arrival.

(The following comments are author's opinions only):

The dates along with the above events that happened on them, give some substance to the fact that, over a ten year period, The Beatles were given four possible opportunities for a reunion. Given also that two of these proposals were for such phenomenal amounts it would probably be true to say that a reunion was never on the cards.

It has long been said over the years that the group were going to get together again in early 1981 to shoot the final scene for their long planned and equally long awaited movie called "The Long and Winding Road". However this has been denied by numerous people, including Beatles expert and author Mark Lewisohn.

Anyway, the facts continue:

April 27th 1981 - Ringo married Barbara Bach. Paul and Linda were on the guest list together with George and Olivia. That evening at the reception in Rags Night Club (London) there was an impromptu 'jam' session - Reunion Number 5?

May 15th 1981 - "All Those Years Ago" (a single from George) was issued. On bass was one James Paul McCartney and on drums Richard Starkey. The song was a tribute to John Lennon.

November 7th 1984 - Guests on the USA television show "Friday Night Video" were interviewed by two new hosts - Lennon (Julian) and McCartney (Paul).

July 12th 1985 - The day before the Live Aid show at Wembley the Sun newspaper ran a cover story "Beatles to re-form for Live Aid" and went on to carry a story about Paul, George, Ringo and Julian Lennon re-forming the group just for the day. Simultaneously the Daily Star newspaper ran "FAB 3 and Lennon's Son for Wembley."

July 13th 1985 - The big day and top of the bill (UK section) was Paul McCartney who sang "Let It Be" backed by (you guessed it!) Pete Townshend, David Bowie, Bob Geldof and Alison Moyet.

Some reunion!

Author's opinions continued:

Every year the Prince's Trust (Patron HRH Prince Charles) hosts a concert at the National Exhibition Centre (NEC) in Birmingham, England. Twice, according to my reckoning, the worlds press has said that there would be a Beatles reunion. The facts show Paul McCartney in 1986 and George Harrison with Ringo Starr in 1987.

1989 - While starting up, an FA Cup semi-final at Hillsborough football ground between Liverpool and Nottingham Forest was stopped because of problems with crowd congestion, in the aftermath 95 people died.

As a tribute to those that died Gerry Marsden (leader of Sixties band Gerry and The Pacemakers) made a suggestion that "Ferry Cross The Mersey" be re-recorded with an all star band. Within 48 hours the newspapers had a story that The Beatles were to re-form for Hillsborough. Much as any fan would like to see the Beatles re-form, it was sickening that the sensationalised reunion rumours were given precedence over other more important issues. At this point we would like to add our own personal tribute to those 95 and their families.

Eric Clapton is the only person who at one time or another has played with Lennon, McCartney, Harrison or Starr (apart from Ringo's earlier stand-ins). Indeed he was even on a Beatles album! But he'd be the first to say "NO" to any further stupid reunion ideas.

"Didn't The Beatles give you everything on God's earth for ten years ...?
- John Lennon 1980

So why to some is that still not enough?

Paul, George and Ringo all still give us great solo records and live shows. Yoko (as the now admired 'Keeper of the Keys') makes sure that the fans are allowed more and more of John's tapes and movies each year. EMI still issue new Beatles Concept albums. With fan clubs around the world all this helps us to remember that unique and fascinating music 'legend' that is THE BEATLES!!

- and "YES" that IS enough ... and thank you for it!

CHAPTER ELEVEN

"IN THE LAP OF THE GODS AND THE HANDS OF THE BEATLES"

WHERE ARE THEY NOW? (All ages at January 1, 1990)

JANE ASHER (43) - Lives in Chelsea with her husband, cartoonist Gerald Scarfe. A successful stage and television actress, she has also written books on designing party cakes and contributes a column to The Independent newspaper.

DEREK TAYLOR (57) - Now lives in Suffolk with his wife Joan and six children. He worked for Warner Brothers Records until 1978, since when he has written and 'ghost' written a number of books including George Harrison's biography "I Me Mine".

GEORGE MARTIN (63) - Owns Air Recording Studios in Monserrat, Caribbean, and is on the board of Chrysalis Records. In 1986-87 he re-mastered The Beatles albums for compact disc release. He is now working on "All You Need Is Ears", a Channel 4 TV show in 24 parts to complement his book of the same name.

CYNTHIA LENNON (49) - Has been divorced 3 times and now lives on the Isle of Man. Involved over the years with fabric and wallpaper design, she also launched her own perfume. She is now joint Manager of "Lennons", a Cafe/Bar in London, but at the time of writing has bought herself out of the management team.

RAVI SHANKAR (69) - Even now he is a much famed musician and continues to give concerts of Sitar music all over the world with his son as a fellow player.

MICHAEL COOPER (R.I.P.) - At the age of 31 he took his own life in March 1973. Leaving a note for his son Adam he (the man responsible for the most famous album sleeve ever - "Sgt. Pepper") said: "I come from what your generation will call the half and half. Some of us were bound to fall by the wayside..." Genesis Books issued "Blinds and Shutters - The Michael Cooper Collection" in November 1989.

YOKO ONO (56) - Now one of the richest women in America, the fans affectionately call her "The Keeper of the Keys" as she administers John's estate. She still lives in New York with her son Sean and is said to be thinking about an autobiography. (Author's note - perhaps she will allow us to write it!)

TONY BARROW (53) - Returned to the North of England eight years ago after running a PR company in London. He is now a freelance showbusiness writer based in Morecombe, Lancashire. He once said - "Between 10 and 15 per cent of what I do is still Beatles related in some way or another."

MAL EVANS (R.I.P.) - Shot dead in January 1976 by Los Angeles police during a dispute where he was mistaken for somebody else. The case was never closed.

NEIL ASPINALL - Still to be found running Apple somewhere in London. Even after all these years nothing is final. In 1988 he suffered a mild heart attack because of the worries and stress. He is currently still trying to finish the documentary on the true Beatles story "Long and Winding Road" of which he is Director.

HUNTER DAVIS (58) - An updated version of his authorised biography was issued in 1985. He works as a journalist for the Sunday Times and has the dubious honour of being the man who has already written The Beatles' obituaries.

PATTI BOYD (44) - Having divorced George in the mid-Seventies she married Eric Clapton, who wrote the songs "Layla" and "Wonderful Tonight" in her honour. Still showing some of that Sixties beauty that made her a top model, she can always be found at showbusiness parties.

PETE BEST (48) - He tried unsuccessfully to take his own life on two occasions in the mid-Sixties, after which Pete settled down and went to work for Liverpool City Council. His book "Beatle" was issued in 1985 and gave a new angle on all the early days of the group in Liverpool and Hamburg. Fame took its time to find Pete Best but since his book he is a regular invited guest at Beatle Conventions worldwide and is always mobbed for autographs and stories.

So what of the Inner Circle - the Four Musketeers - all for one and one for all !

GEORGE HARRISON (46) - Still lives at Friar Park with his second wife Olivia and their son, Dhani aged 11. In 1987 he formed Handmade Films Ltd. to produce such major British films as "Life of Brian", "Time Bandits" and "Mona Lisa". In 1982, after his "Gone Troppo" album, he announced that he was retiring from music for good, only to come back in 1987 with the album "Cloud Nine" and a number one single "Got My Mind On You". He then joined the rock supergroup The Travelling Wilburys in 1988 and is now said to be working on a double "Greatest Hits" compilation for Warner Bros.

RINGO STARR (49) - Is now living in Berkshire with his second wife, ex-Bond girl Barbara Bach. He additionally owns a commercial recording studio and a market garden. More recently he has gained a new audience of fans (under fives) as the voice of Thomas The Tank Engine. Following career-long problems, he (and wife Barbara) entered the Betty Ford Clinic for Alcoholics in 1989 and were successfully discharged a few weeks later. Ringo has since decided to throw himself back into his music and is now halfway through an American tour of his Greatest Hits under the title "Ringo and His All-Starr Band".

PAUL McCARTNEY (47) - Has a home in Sussex with his wife Linda. He has remained as successful a solo artist as he was a Beatle, having recently worked (with Elvis Costello) on his fifteenth solo
album "Flowers In The Dirt". A number of the albums were issued with his band Wings, containing mainly Paul, Linda and ex-Moody Blues man Denny Lane, and he is currently on his first world tour since 1976. He has also recently issued an album of old Rock 'n Roll Standards in Russia (titled "Chobba b CCCP") as his effort towards Glasnost.

And finally ... Seeing as the story has been told so many times (and we all know what happened anyway) for the sake of the book and in tribute to his memory, let's just say ...

"Thank you for the music ... we'll never forget you!"

JOHN LENNON 1940 - 1980 (Rest In Peace)

Paul McCARTNEY and FREINDS of the EARTH.

The last world tour Paul ever did was in 1976,since which time every Magazine,T.V.Show,Radio Programme or Newspaper that has a gossip spot has told it;s public that Paul would be back on the road that very same year.

In 1980 with the death of John Lennon,it looked more like a firm seal on Paul never touring again,however with Bob Geldofs Live Aid in 1984,Paul was coaxed into closing the U.K.section of the show.A later appearance on the Princes Trust Rock Gala at the Birmingham NEC gave Paul the confidence to "Get Back" to live performances,after all this was an entirely new audience out there,to whom the chance of seeing their live hero was a dream come true.

In the gap between Pauls last world tour and 1989 the rock world had seen one major change in high profile tours-simply Sponsorship,with Micheal Jackson it was Pepsi,with Madonna it was Cola but with an ex Beatle,who had supported more realistic causes in the sixties likeLove and Peace a tour of this size had to carry a message.

You only have to open your newspaper to know that the world of the eighties and nineties is in bad shape,but some of whats gone wrong can be put right,it's not to late to change.

Indeed with the help of Freinds of the Earth,we could just save the planet,read on and see what you think.

The Earth needs all the friends it can get. And it needs them now.

For thousands upon thousands of years our planet has sustained a wonderfully rich tapestry of life. Now, one single species — humankind — is putting the Earth at risk.

People the world over are suffering the effects of pollution, deforestation and radiation. Species are disappering at a terrifying rate. The warming of the atmosphere threatens us all with devastating changes in climate and food production.

It needn't be like this. We know enough to reverse the damage, and to manage the Earth's astonishing wealth more fairly and sustainably. But the political will to bring about such a transformation is still lacking.

And that's exactly where Friends of the Earth comes in. Isn't it time you joined us?

Friends of the Earth is one of the leading environmental pressure groups in the UK. Established in 1971, FoE now has more than 270 active local groups in England and Wales, 170,000 supporters and a separate organisation in Scotland. FoE's role is to persuade politicians and decision makers at every level that only by protecting the Earth can we protect ourselves — against pollution and the destruction of our urban and rural environments. FoE campaigns on 12 major issues, including Global Warming, Tropical Rainforests, Water and Air Pollution, Energy, The Ozone Layer and Recycling.

Friends of the Earth, 26-28 Underwood Street, London N1 7JQ

IN THE
LAP OF THE GODS
AND THE
HANDS OF THE BEATLES

RADIO SERIES

"WHY A RADIO SERIES?"

What makes a normal, healthy, happily married fifty-year-old suddenly decide to make a radio series about a group who not only broke up twenty years ago, but have been done by various broadcasting organisations around the world to the point of boredom?

The "last straw that broke the camel's back" was the conceit of a well-known broadcasting station who had the nerve to make a series of programmes on how it lost its precious Beatle tapes, go into great detail as to its foolishness in doing so — "Oh dear, we've lost the only copy of John and Paul's thingummyjig!" — and then ensure that they got an award for so doing!

I joined the BBC in 1958 as an engineer in Manchester and became a Studio Manager (sound mixer, sound effects etc.) in London in 1960. Such was the interest in pop music, pop culture and every innovation of the swinging sixties that my career progression was meteoric. I graduated from sound effects on Mrs Dale's Diary, Beyond Our Ken, Round The Horne, Navy Lark etc, playing discs, sorry gramophone records! on the Jack Jackson Show (the original Adrian Juste), Housewives' Choice, Family Favourites and Saturday Club to actual sound mixing with the Joe Loss Orchestra, Bob Miller Band, and Mantovani.

Early in 1963 Pop Go The Beatles arrived on the air waves. The first sound mixer on this programme was a wonderful chap called Charles Clark-Maxwell who was a former pupil of Eton. As far as John and Ringo were concerned he might as well have been an ex-Martian as an ex-Etonian, such were the language difficulties.

It was decided, therefore, that as I came from somewhere "up north" I should do the rest of the series. Paul McCartney still refers to me as "our translator".

From this beginning I went on to mix "From Us To You" for producer Bryan Marriot and all the well-known acts of the sixties including the Hollies, with whom I had a special affinity as I had been playing in a Manchester group in 1957 prior to my joining the Beeb as the Hollies were starting out; the Rolling Stones, Gerry and the Pacemakers, the Searchers, the Fourmost, the Tremeloes, Freddy and the

Dreamers, Herman's Hermits, the Troggs, the Animals, Dave Dee, Cliff Richard and the Shadows, Marty Wilde, Kiki Dee, Dusty Springfield, Gene Pitney, Tom Jones, Englebert Humperdinck, the late Roy Orbison, Del Shannon...I could go on; I often do.

As a result of my experience when BBC-2 opened in 1964 I mixed, live from the Royal Albert Hall, Top Beat, produced by Robin Scott, later to become Controller of Radio One.

Top Beat was basically impossible! Fifty-one microphones to fiddle with, six rock groups, one big band, one jazz band and six vocal microphones. We managed it, but I'd hate to hear it now.

However, in typical BBC manner, when you have found your true vocation (mine was mixing) the powers that be promote you, so I was made a Light Programme (forerunner of Radio One) producer. I quickly found myself "up to my neck" in cinema organs, old time dance bands and jazz trios, but then took over the Beatles Bank Holiday Special from Bryan Marriot, who was, by then, up to HIS neck in jazz! I changed "From Us To You" into "Ticket To Ride" which was to run until the Beatles' last ever broadcast in 1965.

When Radio One eventually turned into a sausage machine of mediocraty (as it still is) around 1968 and innovative ideas put forward by young, talented producers Malcolm Brown, Bev Philips, Bernie Andrews, Bill Bebb, Roger Purey and myself, were all firmly squashed I felt it was time to leave and although that decision was taken for me the BBC and I parted company in April 1970, strangely enough the same month that the Beatles broke up.

There will now be a twenty year intermission. Around the end of 1988 I was telephoned, out of the blue, by Kevin Howlett of the BBC and asked if I would contribute to the "Beeb's Lost Beatle Tapes" to be broadcast later in the year. I readily agreed and actually got paid for it.

After twenty years I had got the taste for broadcasting again and when I met Alan G. Parker, together we planned the definitive radio show, "In the Lap of the Gods and the Hands of the Beatles". Paul McCartney was enthusiastic and gave us his blessing.

The initial result was a fairly Radio Three approach to a brilliant group. No record identification, no back announcements, no voice overs, no controversy; just facts, music and interviews, some not heard before.

Unfortunately after speaking to various high-flying American radio network executives the approach we had originally envisaged was, not to put too fine a point on it, considered unsuitable for US markets.

The resultant new radio series is back announced, voice-overed and snappy. In other words...yes, Radio One-ish!

Oh well, this is where I came in!

BEATLES FAN MAGAZINES

(SAE for reply)

LENNON INTERNATIONAL: 1 Wellington Ave, St Ives, Cambs. PE17 6UT England
THE BEATLES BOOK: 45 St Mary's Road, Ealing, London W5 5RQ, England
DAY TRIPPER: 25 Chapel House Road, Nelson, Lancs. BB9 9DJ, England
BEATLES UNLIMITED: PO Box 602, 3420 AP Nieuwegein, Holland
BEATLE FAN: PO Box 33515, Decatur, GA 30033, USA
BEATLES LONDON: Flat 4, Oaklands, Constance Rd, Whitton, Middlesex, England
CAVERN CITY TOURS: 4th Floor, 31 Matthew Street, Liverpool 2, England
BEATLES SHOP: 31 Matthew Street, Liverpool 2, England
GOOD DAY SUNSHINE: 397 Edgewood Avenue, Newhaven CT 06511, USA
BEATLE FEST: PO Box 436, Westwood NJ 07675, USA
BEATLE MUSEUM: 456 Seymour Street, Vancouver BC, Canada, V6B 3H1
PEPPERLAND: 9326 W.Katella Avenue, Anaheim, CA 92804
BEATLES NYTT: 10 Arsjubile Bar, Med Att GE UT, Sitt 60:E, Germany
WINGS FAN CLUB: PO Box 4UP, London W1A 4UP, England
BVL: 53 Mead Avenue, Langley, Slough, Berks. SL3 8HS, England

THE BOOTLEG BEATLES
A BRIEF HISTORY

The Bootleg Beatles were formed in March 1980 by the London Cast of the Broadway Stage Musical 'Beatlemania', after the Show closed in the West End. The first years were spent touring clubs and colleges in the U.K. so it wasn't until 1982 and a sixty date concert tour of the U.S.S.R. that the Band received international acclaim.

More big tours followed, including; India (1983), The Far East (1983, where the Group pulled in 18,000 people at the Areneta Colosseurs ... their biggest audience to date), and the U.S.A. (1984), to commemorate the 20th anniversary of the 'Fab Fours' invasion in 1964.

The sound-alike quality of the Group soon interested the T.V. and film industry and the Band were quickly called upon to recreate Beatles or Beatles-style music for a number of projects. Credits include; the title music for Nick Roeg's film 'Track 29', (Mother), and the signature tune for BBC1's sitcom, 'Help!), as well as countless jingles and advertising inserts.

Now nearly ten years on, the Bootleg Beatles continue to cover the world. This year alone the Band will have performed in twelve countries, from festivals in Belgium and Holland, to concerts in Sri Lanka and Borneo. Their success and durability proving one thing - The Beatles and their music will never die.

NEIL HARRISON-JOHN
Place of Birth: West Kirby, Merseyside.
Date of Birth: 4/12/50
Instruments:Guitar/Keyboards.

Neil began a full time career in music in 1969, since which time he has recorded two albums for Decca and composed a US top twenty hit for Lulu. A founder member of the Bootleg Beatles he successfully auditioned for the part of John in the stage musical BEATLEMANIA in London's West End in December 1979. He is the only Bootleg to have performed with a real Beatle ... This was an 'impromptu gig' with Paul McCartney in the hallway of Paul's fathers house near Liverpool, Christmas eve 1968. He is married with two children and lives in West London. Hobbies include script writing, playing squash, and watching Woody Allen films.

ANDRÉ BARREAU-GEORGE
Place of Birth: London
Date of Birth: 16/4/56
Instruments: Guitar/sitar/harmonica

André, a Beatle fan ever since his Grandmother gave him the 'Twist & Shout' EP for his 7th Birthday, probably has the largest collection of Beatle records south of the Mersey. The other founder member of the 'Bootlegs' he spent two years at the BBC as a programme researcher before being recruited to play George in BEATLEMANIA on the West End Stage. As well as 'Beatling', André also does session work and has recently backed Wreckless Eric on a British tour. He is married and lives in Bayswater, West London and his hobbies include art and impersonations.

RICK ROCK-RINGO
Place of Birth: Kansas, USA
Date of Birth: 2/2/55
Instruments: Drums

Although from 'Missouri-side and not 'Merseyside' Rick has been a Ringo fan since the Beatles first tour in the States. In fact he is the only group member to have actually seen the Beatles live. (In Kansas 1965). He has always played in bands on both sides of the Atlantic, most recently Sham 69 and the Wanderers, and joined the Bootleg Beatles in 1981. He is married with a son and lives in West London. Hobbies include collecting Coca-Cola artifacts of all descriptions and drinking Coca-Cola.

PAUL COOPER-PAUL
Place of Birth: Liverpool
Date of Birth:27/12/59
Instruments: Bass Guitar

The only true 'scouser' Paul lives within walking distance of both John Lennons and Paul McCartneys original South Liverpool homes. Before joining the Bootlegs in 1987, Paul played in several popular Liverpool groups including Mojo Filter and the Famous Game, and even shared the stage with Tony Sheridan and Pete Best in Hamburg. He is single, still lives in Liverpool, and is a regular on the 4.45 to Euston. Favourite hobbies include Football and Football.

SINGLES

1962 - 1970
(U.K. RELEASE DATES)

Label - Parlophone/Apple (*)   Distributor EMI (UK) Ltd
1. LOVE ME DO/P.S.I LOVE YOU 5th October 1962
2. PLEASE PLEASE ME / ASK ME WHY 11th January 1963
3. FROM ME TO YOU / THANK YOU GIRL 12th April 1963
4. SHE LOVES YOU / I'LL GET YOU 23rd August 1963
5. I WANT TO HOLD YOU HAND / THIS BOY 29th November 1963
6. CAN'T BUY ME LOVE / YOU CAN'T DO THAT 20th March 1964
7. HARD DAY'S NIGHT / THINGS WE SAID TODAY 10th July 1964
8. I FEEL FINE / SHE'S A WOMAN 27th November 1964
9. TICKET TO RIDE / YES IT IS 9th April 1965
10. HELP / I'M DOWN 23rd July 1965
11. WE CAN WORK IT OUT / DAY TRIPPER 3rd December 1965
12. PAPERBACK WRITER / RAIN 10th June 1966
13. YELLOW SUBMARINE / ELEANOR RIGBY 5th August 1966
14. STRAWBERRY FIELDS / PENNY LANE 17th February 1967
15. ALL YOU NEED IS LOVE / BABY YOU'RE A RICH MAN 7th July 1967
16. HELLO GOODBYE / I AM THE WALRUS 24th November 1967
17. LADY MADONNA / THE INNER LIGHT 15th March 1968
18. HEY JUDE / REVOLUTION * 30th August 1968
19. GET BACK / DON'T LET ME DOWN * 11th April 1969
20. BALLAD OF JOHN 'N YOKO / OLD BROWN SHOE * 30th May 1969
21. SOMETHING / COME TOGETHER * 31st October 1969
22. LET IT BE / YOU KNOW MY NAME * 6th March 1970

All of the above are now also available as 3" CD singles but because EMI issued them as 20th Anniversary Picture Discs they are Limited Editions and only available while stocks last.

AFTER 1970
(EMI U.K. RELEASE DATES)

1. BACK IN THE USSR / OB LA DI OB LA DA
2. YESTERDAY / ACT NATURALLY
3. SGT. PEPPER*WITH A LITTLE HELP FROM MY FRIENDS / A DAY IN THE LIFE
4. BEATLES MOVIE MEDLEY / I'M HAPPY JUST TO DANCE WITH YOU.

ALBUMS

AFTER 1970
(EMI U.K. RELEASE DATES)

1962 - 1966 (DOUBLE) 20th April 1973
1967 - 1970 (DOUBLE) 20th April 1973
ROCK 'N ROLL MUSIC (DOUBLE) 11th June 1976
LIVE AT THE HOLLYWOOD BOWL 6th May 1977
LOVE SONGS (DOUBLE) 28th November 1977
BEATLES COLLECTION (14 ALBUM BOX SET) 15th December 1978
RARITIES (FREE WITH BOX SET) 1st October 1979
BEATLES BALLADS 1st October 1980
REEL MUSIC (PLUS FREE BOOK) 12th March 1982
FROM LIVERPOOL (8 ALBUM BOX SET) 1st October 1980

and what about those American Capitol Albums we mentioned ...?

AMERICAN CAPITOL ALBUMS

MEET THE BEATLES 20th January 1964
SECOND ALBUM 10th April 1964
HARD DAYS NIGHT 26th June 1964
SOMETHING NEW 20th July 1964
BEATLES STORY (DOUBLE) 23rd November 1964
BEATLES '65 15th December 1964
EARLY BEATLES 22nd April 1965
BEATLES VI 14th June 1965
HELP 13th August 1965
RUBBER SOUL 6th December 1965
YESTERDAY AND TODAY 20th June 1966
RARITIES 24th March 1980

NB: All the albums from "Sgt. Pepper" to "Let It Be" were issued in the USA at the same time and in the same format as UK versions.

RECOMMENDED UK VIDEO VIEWING
(VHS ONLY)

HARD DAYS NIGHT VESTRON VIDEO
YELLOW SUBMARINE WARNER HOME VIDEO
COMPLEAT BEATLES MGM/VA HOME VIDEO
IMAGINE (JOHN LENNON) WARNER HOME VIDEO
RAGE (4 HOURS) PRIVATE REEL

ALBUMS

ORIGINAL UK ALBUMS

A FEW YOU HAVEN'T SEEN

AND NOW WE'RE LEAVING!!!

"IN THE LAP OF THE GOD'S AND IN THE HANDS OF THE BEATLES"

ACKNOWLEDGEMENTS

Our sincere thanks to the following who were instrumental in assisting us to get this book to you, the reader, marginally before we were considered by families and friends as being close to insanity - having spent uncountable hours of innumerable days and nights on Coke (the drink!) and Chinese take aways!

Jo Pratt, Perry Anderson - EMI UK; Frances Osman - Polydor; Linda Heyen (for keeping us up to date with the USA); Dave 'n Bill Cavern City Tours (for keeping it alive); Steve 'n Paul - Beatles Shop (without whom ...); Petra Zeitz (for proving that we're not the only ones who will stand for hours just to see a Beatle); Mark Lapidos (Beatle Fest USA); the Astonishing Neil Kinder (for putting the music in my collection); Martin Cobb (hands across the water); Valeriy Onishchenko (Back in the USSR); Woody (for sticking by when others didn't - a friend); Rex Features; Beat Publications; Audrey Francois (at MPL); Neil and his team (at Apple); Stan (you can't wipe this one); Caroline Turbefield,Cris(at Reidys for starting Alan off),Mum and Dad and families (for putting up with us - it can only get worse folks); Brian Rowlands and Anne Simmons; Keith Badman (the Vision is yours); all Fan Club members (this one's for you) and finally last but not least ...

to DOCTOR WINSTON O'BOOGIE (name used by John on his '75 Rock 'n Roll Album), APOLLO C. VERMOUTH (name used by Paul when producing Bonzo Dog Do Da Band), HARRI O'GEORGERSON (name used by George as a guest on Eric Clapton Album) and OGNIR RRATS
(name used by Ringo in Prince and Pauper TV special) for being there when music, and the world, needed you!

ADDITIONAL INFORMATION.
Archway Publishing
BCM:-BOX 3595,
LONDON WC1 3XX.

EMI Music/Album Enquiries:
EMI Music (UK) Ltd.,
EMI House,
20 Manchester Square,
London W1, England
(Phone 01 468 4488)

Book/Radio Series/Other Enquiries
David F. Bowles/Keith Bateson,
Bateson-Bowles Ltd.,
14 Dryburgh Avenue,
Bolton,
Lancashire, BL1 6PA
England
(Phone 0204 57071)